The Journey to Canaan

How to Deal with the Contradictions, Crooks and Bends on the Road of Life

W. F. Washington, Sr. Ph.D.

The Journey to Canaan

How to Deal with the Contradictions, Crooks and Bends on the Road of Life

Christian Living Books
An Imprint of Pneuma Life Publishing
Largo, MD

Copyright © 2002 W. F. Washington, Sr.

Christian Living Books, Inc.
An imprint of Pneuma Life Publishing
P. O. Box 7584
Largo, MD 20792
301-218-9092
info@christianlivingbooks.com
www.christianlivingbooks.com

All rights reserved under the international copyright law. No part of this book may be reproduced or transmitted in any form or by any means, electronic or mechanical, including photocopying, recording, or by any information storage and retrieval system, without the express, written permission of the publisher.

Printed in the United States of America

ISBN 0-9716240-1-1

Unless otherwise indicated, all Scripture quotations are taken from the King James Version of the Bible.

"A Theological Interpretation"

"Because of the sovereignty of God, this book will show how a tribe of nomads changed the way modern man thinks and feels theologically."

Contents

preface i
acknowledgments v
introduction vii
- The Greatest Journey–The Journey of Life
- The Journey to Canaan
- The God of the Canaan Road

chapter I: .... page 1
RULES OF THE CANAAN ROAD
- Stay in Your Lane
- Keep Your Eyes on the Road
- Obey the Speed Limit

chapter II: .... page 29
LIFE'S DILEMMAS — DETOURS, DEAD ENDS & DRY PLACES
- A Detour Dilemma
- A Deadly Dead End
- A Demonstrative Dry Place

chapter III: .... page 53
WHY LIFE'S DETOURS, DEAD ENDS AND DRY PLACES?
- That You May Live
- That You May Remember
- Spiritual Concept for Acquiring Wealth
- Fortification for Detours, Dead Ends and Dry Places
- Heart Matters

chapter IV: page 79
JORDAN RIVER—A PRECURSOR TO CANAAN

- The Preacher–Prophet and His Purpose as Provocateur
- God's Challenge to the Preacher–Prophet Provocateur
  - *The Call to Claim the Lord*
  - *The Call to Have Confidence in the Lord*
  - *The Call to Carry out the Law*
  - *The Call to Courage in Leadership*
- The Preacher–Prophet Provocateur Challenges the People
  - *The Challenge to Readiness*
  - *The Challenge to Responsibility*
- The People's Response to the Preacher–Prophet Provocateur
  - *They Commit Themselves to a Life of Surrender*
  - *They Commit Themselves to a Life of Submission*
  - *They Commit Themselves to a Life of Separation*
- Preparing for an Ocular Display of Divinity
  - *The Parting and Passage Through a Perilous River*

chapter v: page 105
THE TERRESTRIAL VS. THE TEMPORAL AND TEMPORARY TESTIMONY OF THE TENANCY OF GOD

- They Who are Ark-Led are Well-Led
- Not Timid nor Terrified About Terra Firma

chapter vi: page 115
THE THEOLOGICAL AND TRANSITIONAL SHIFT DEMANDED FROM DEEP AND CHILLY JORDAN

- Doubt and Fear to Favor and Faith
- Hope to Certainty
- Grudges and Accusations to Forgiving and Reconciliation

- Physicality to Spirituality
- What are You Laboring for to What are You Living for
- Confusing and Doubting to Certainty and Trust

chapter VII: page 131
JORDAN RIVER—CHILLY, DEEP AND COLD

- It Involved a Challenge
  - *Watch God*
  - *Follow God*
  - *Honor God*
- It Involved a Command
- It Involved a Commitment

chapter VIII: page 145
THE ANATOMY OF THE JORDAN RIVER CROSSING

- There was a Problem
- There was a Plan
- There was a Performance

chapter IX: page 157
PREPARING TO CONFRONT THE "ITES" ON THE ROAD TO CANAAN

- Overview: Israel Post Jordan Assignment
- A Rhema Word Extrapolation
  - *The Difficulties of Life as Anxiously Dreaded by Us*
  - *The Difficulties of Life Graciously Anticipated and provided by God*
  - *Nations, Like Individuals May Become Incorrigible*
  - *The Israelites were Sent into Canaan to Establish the True Worship of God*

chapter x:
CONFRONTING THE "ITES" ON THE ROAD TO CANAAN
page 167
- Hittites: "Fear, Dread, Terror"
- Girgashites: "Dwellers on the Safe Soil"
- Amorites: "Mouthy, Talkers"
- Canaanites: "Dwellers in the Lowplace"
- Perizzites: "Squatters"
- Hivites: "Wicked, Hypocritical"
- Jebusites: "A Threshing Place"

chapter xi:
POSSESSING CANAAN'S POSSESSIONS
page 193
- The "I Wills" of Christ
- A Self Concept Mainspring of Our Christian Possession
- Life Storms vs. Christian Possessions
- Nine Things You Should Know About Storms
- Relevancy and Identity—A Christian Crisis

chapter xii:
HITCHHIKING ON THE ROAD TO CANAAN
page 209
- Thumbing a Ride
- The Hitchhiker and Koinonia
- The Varacity of Thumbing

epilogue

Preface

Saints and soldiers of God all across this nation are struggling to be all that they can be in Christ Jesus. They are acutely aware of their inner strivings and bio-psychosocial propensities in their daily walk with the Lord. Because of these innate, normal and human tendencies, their struggle escalates. The escalation of these intrinsic and extrinsic forces demands a fundamental need for a tupos, a methodology to deal with them.

As the marching army of God seeks to move ever forward, His soldiers need a rudder, a compass to guide them during the times of adversity. If the soldiers of God are to move methodically in their walk in righteousness and victory, a biblical strategy must be found.

This book seeks to extract a strategy from the second and fifth book of Moses and the first few chapters of Joshua. From the Exodus and the Deuteronomonic literature, a link will be established with Israel. I will take the position that Israel's journey to Canaan is our journey. I will postulate that God in His essential being and sovereignty is the same. The struggles faced by ancient Israel are essentially the same struggles faced by every Christian soldier today. I will show that in this journey of Israel there were problems. However, for their problems, God had a plan. To the degree that they followed the divine plan in performance of it, was to that degree that they succeeded!

They went their way from the Exodus, through the wilderness, through the Red Sea, and eventually crossed over the Jordan River into Canaan. The Christian creed, the New Testament, refers unequivocally to the journey to Canaan.

"Now ALL THESE THINGS happened unto THEM for EXAMPLES: and they are written for OUR ADMONITION, upon whom the ends of the world are come." (Emphasis mine)

It does not matter how long one has been in sin; what matters is whether one has lost his or her desire to be emancipated. The period of bondage began for God's people Israel when they entered into Egypt. This period lasted for 430 years; during this period, an initial family of seventy-five souls increased into a great and formidable nation. The author will postulate that the shadows of the Old Testament became the substance and reality of the new covenant.

This book speaks directly to each Christian individually as well as the church collectively. If the postulates herein given are accepted and internalized by faith, Canaan will be achieved. This book can be reduced generally to six principles, which are woven throughout the book.

1. *Forget the Past*
2. *Grasp God's Vision*
3. *Watch God*
4. *Follow God*
5. *Honor God*
6. *Obey God*

This book is a combination of a sermon and lecture series that I have taught and preached across the country titled, "Ites on the Road to Canaan." Thousands have been strengthened, lives have been changed, and hundreds have been baptized. I am convinced that this ancient story (4,000 years before Christ) sets a noble example for strength and character.

It will be encouraging for the readers of this book to know that the principles postulated herein are biblical. The extrapolations are rhema words derived from the Divine Logos word. It takes literally the word of the venerable apostle Paul in his letter to the church at Rome. He writes:

"For whatsoever things were written aforetime were written for our learning, that we through patience and comfort of the scriptures might have hope."—Rom. 15:4

Jesus, the Pre-Existing Logos, the Messianic Perusal, the Eschatological Anticipation of the Cosmos, spoke also to this question in John 5:39. We read:

"[Ye] Search the scriptures; for in them ye think ye have eternal life: and they are THEY WHICH TESTIFY OF ME." (Emphasis mine)

Again, the Master speaks to the question of the validity of the ancient text. In John 7:38, we read:

"He that believeth on me, as the SCRIPTURE hath said, out of his belly shall flow rivers of living water."

The journey to Canaan is a microscopic view of what the author calls the journey of life. This position is vouchsafed by the fact that ancient Israel is a type of God's new Israel. Their journey is our journey. Their God is our God. He who led them, leads us. That being so, the construct of this book is intended as a Christian guide for all who have embarked on the Canaan road with a view of finally entering the Promised Land.

This book is about dead ends, detours, personal storms, and dry places, and how they can be handled successfully. The key to overcoming life's detours, dead ends, storms, and dry places depends on the ability to allow God to lead and guide us through them. To the degree that we understand these divine elements of deity, it will be to that degree we make the journey to Canaan safely.

This book will answer the often asked question: "Why does God allow detours, dead ends, storms, and dry places in our lives?" Do unexplainable things happen in our lives based solely on happenstance, or does it go to the question of the divine purpose of God?

This book is about a river called Jordan. It runs chilly, deep and cold and it must be crossed in order to attain our Canaan. There will be Jordan rivers in our lives that will stand between us and where we need to go. I will show how to cross your Jordan and make it roll back and stand up in a heap. I will discuss the need for every saint of God to observe the "Rules of the Road." To successfully navigate the Canaan road, absolute obedience to the rules, stop signs and speed limits must be studiously observed.

Finally, this book will expose and show the seven enemies that confronted Israel–enemies which will confront us on our Canaan odyssey. These enemies are greater and mightier than we are. They will not be defeated by human efforts. It will only be through divine intervention that they will be ultimately defeated.

The final chapter will deal with "Hitchhikers on the Road to Canaan." I will show that, when we are not able to hitch a ride on this road, the distance from our Egypt to Canaan will be overwhelming and in many instances fatal.

Acknowledgments

First and foremost, I thank God of whose I am, and whom I serve for His mercy and grace. It is because of His long-suffering and love that I have been spared for this volume. I make no boast of originality. The words appearing in this volume are a compilation of sermons, lectures and seminars I have done across the nation. I stipulate that no real effort in time is without roots somewhere else.

I am grateful to the saints of God at the Figueroa church in Los Angeles and the Harlem church in New York. They encouraged me to put these lectures in print.

To my baby daughter Soncyarai, who did much of the typing of the original draft. Finally, to my wife Deloris, who allowed me to write without ever complaining of lack of attention. And, to all the unnamed persons of whom I have hitched a ride on my journey to Canaan.

–W. F. Washington, Sr.

Introduction

We are all on a journey, whether we like it or not. For most, that journey begins at birth and ends in death. But to the Christian traveler who has come to know God, the journey is more complex. Those two basic road markers, birth and death, from the womb to the tomb, remain in place. Yet they are supplemented by others and are seen in a different light to those who embark on the Canaan odyssey.

Those of us who have embarked on this Canaan odyssey, if we are faithful, have a sense of the beyond. We sense that somewhere over the horizon exists something yet unknown and unseen. Commensurate with that sense is a belief that it offers us the spiritual satisfaction and fulfillment that has eluded us in this life.

It is the same sense that beats in the hearts of the world's first explorers during the age of exploration. They believed and were convinced that new worlds lay beyond the horizon. It was that faith that would not allow them to be satisfied until they had discovered and explored them.

Many, who have begun on this Canaan odyssey and have turned aside, suffer not from the failure of the Christian faith or Christianity as a system, but claim dissatisfaction with Christianity. But it is really dissatisfaction with something else—their own personal grasp of Christianity? The problem lies in the definition and understanding a life—the life of the Christ of God.

The greatest biblical journey, in the author's opinion, is the journey of God's people Israel. Even the Exodus of God's people Israel tells our story. Each of us has a personal journey to make, from our own Egypt to our promised land. We all have left something behind in order to make this journey. We all have had to break free from our former lives to begin afresh. We were in Egypt. We were delivered from bondage. We are to some degree still in the wilderness, on our way to the Promised Land.

The story of the Exodus involves us, because it is about us. The reader can therefore enter these pages and upon this narrative knowing that this is our story. We belong in it, and it belongs in us. It is all part of the history of our redemption, of which we are a part.

This volume is a call to the reader to use the framework of the Canaan odyssey from Egypt to the Promised Land and to make sense of our personal pilgrimage of faith. I hasten to add a note to the reader that the Canaan odyssey is not a journey that needs to necessarily be foreboded. We do not embark on the Canaan odyssey alone. There are untold numbers of saints of God, past and present, who have navigated this road. They are part and parcel of the gracious provision of God by which He enables us to achieve what He purposes and promises.

I need to be clear here: the author is not saying that being a Christian and navigating the road to Canaan is simply a replication of what other saints have done or thought. Each life of faith is completely original and is grounded in the unique identity of each believer. There is much we can learn from those who have gone on before us. But in the final analysis, we have to get on with the business of the Canaan road and not just read books about what others thought and did. We can, however, filter their insight and foresight through the lens of our own lives and allow them to come into focus on our journey on the road to Canaan. This concept will be enlarged in the chapter "Hitchhiking on the Road to Canaan."

It must be clear that no one can make this journey for us, or on our behalf. We must walk the lonesome valley by ourselves. There are no surrogates in the life of faith. Yet, there will be help provided by divine intervention and fellowship with others who will be our fellow travelers. We must prepare, starting even as you read these pages. We must step up to the plate, use our personal imagination to build a mindset that will succor us in making sense of the great journey that lies before us—the Canaan odyssey. We need a mindset that will capture the spiritual landmarks along the way, the obstacles we shall meet, the safe havens where we may shelter, sources of food and water, and above all, the destination—which is our goal!

The aim of this volume is to draw on the rudders of those ancient sages who have been there before and who wait patiently for us to reach the finishing line with anticipatory glee. This volume further makes the assumption that, as saints of God, Christians are frail, fragile, and fallible, and exposed to and go through the deep human valleys of life. It further postulates that going through our deep valleys of life would not be nearly as frustrating if we had some kind of method and strategy for the trip.

First, human valley navigation is not so bad if we have a strong mindset, and we have been assured previously that we would make it all right. Our success in human valley travels will depend on the wherewithal we have to get us through.

Secondly, we can navigate our human valleys with steadfastness if we believe whom it was that told us "we could make it." Human valleys in life are not permanent stations. They will loom before us, deep, dark, dreary and devastating, but they are to be traveled "through." When we find ourselves in our valleys we must not stop! We must walk through them. To the degree that we have a "strong mindset," to the degree that we believe in Him who has assured us safe passage, it is to that degree that our valley sojourn will not be as painstaking and frustratingly antagonizing.

Saints of God are endowed with an "aboveness" that is received at conversion (Col. 3:1). In addition to this aboveness, saints receive a "blessedness" that equips them for the journey to Canaan. To be merely told that one has an aboveness and a blessedness but not told how to use these virtues as a modus operandi to stabilize, structure and balance the chaos and crises in our lives, is to live beneath our glorious privilege.

It is the opinion of the writer that members of the Church of Christ are to have a strategy for standstill and human valley travel. All of us, one time or the other, will come to a standstill in life, meaning, a place in our living when we do not know what to do. I have counseled hundreds of saints as a minister and as a psychologist. All have at least one thing in common: they wished to know "What do I do when I do not know what to do?"

In the kingdom of God, I have found that we are woefully lacking in our teaching. Where it pertains to the whole field of practical Christian living and biblical guidelines for dealing with the day-to-day pressures of life, we fall short. With this awareness, I resolved to write this volume. I have been led by my spirit to do this special volume on Canaan and the will of God for our lives.

The Canaan odyssey demonstrates that the Lord does not bring his people to a place to leave them. He is present in every aspect of our lives. To not clearly understand and perceive God's will, will eventuate in a "theological smallness" that will ultimately characterize our fellowship and behavior.

A cursory and careful look at our local congregations will show that our Sunday schools, worship assemblies, Bible classes and youth programs are numerically small, to say the least. It is a truism that, to the small mind, even God Himself is small. What is God's will for our lives? What is God's will for our congregation? While these may be elementary questions, they go to the question of attitude. This volume on Canaan will show that attitude affects our will, and our will determines our spiritual mobility and durability.

The author will show that the Christian road to spiritual Canaan is paved with distractions that must not be discounted, but dealt with, and that we are not left to deal with these distractions alone. God has provided weapons, methods, strategies, and guidelines with which to fight and conquer the enemy. While this will be a biblical prescription that assures us of reaching our spiritual Canaan, there is also another dimension to this volume.

Canaan may very well represent secular goals. Any legitimate goal—a career, education, family unity, marriage, or abundant living—can be styled or seen as our Canaan. In the pursuit of any Canaan, there will be hindrances, valleys, and tempestuous seas, but I am convinced we can get there. What is Canaan for if you could not get there?

In this volume on Canaan and its travel, we will follow the sojourn of God's people Israel. In this grand old story from the ancient page we will see that millions of Israelites who left Egypt did not reach Canaan. It was not because it was unreachable or unattainable, but because Israel did not follow the "Rules of the Road."

This volume is a call to the adult Christian as well as the young Christian to observe the rules of the road as God gave them. All who would dare follow these rules will, as did Joshua and Caleb, reach Canaan, the land that flowed with milk and honey.

It is the hope of the author that you will read this volume and have your faith renewed and your heart and soul energized, knowing that you are not alone in your situation, knowing that weapons will be formed against you, but also knowing that they will not prosper. The intent is to alert you to the knowledge that "situations," whether they are positive or negative, are not necessarily a bad thing. Situations might well be a "set up." That is, God may have something different in mind for you. It could well be that the intent of God is to work His will in your life. We must not allow situations, whatever they may be, to deter us from reaching our Canaan.

A case in point would be an incident in the life of Abraham, the father of the faithful. God instructed him to take his son and sacrifice him on Mount Moriah. Clearly, God had something in mind for Abraham, but he had to create a "situation" in the life of Abraham to bring it about. Abraham, clearly, did not fully understand the strange request and resulting situation that obviously came directly from God. God wanted Abraham to see something he had not seen before. He had seen God as El Shaddai, but he had not seen God as Jehovahjireh (God will provide). So He created a situation wherein Abraham was able to see clearly that God would provide a ram or way out.

Situations we may face on the Canaan odyssey are not to be dreaded necessarily. It is through situations that we come to truly know others and ourselves. In Chapter II, I will enlarge this concept, showing why God leads us into certain situations. The journey to Canaan is a long and arduous one, but if we allow God to lead, our Canaans will be assured. In I Cor. 10:13, we read:

"There hath no temptation taken you but such as is common to man: but God is faithful, who WILL not suffer you to BE TEMPTED ABOVE that ye are able; but will with the temptation also make a way TO escape, that ye may be ABLE to bear it." (Emphasis mine)

The Greatest Journey–The Journey of Life

This story of the ancient people of God is one of faith, doubt, and a mixture of hope and despair. The residuals and theological fallouts from this amazing story reach into the fabrics of the twenty-first century more than 4,000 years later.

From the cradle to the grave, life is a journey. It is not only a journey, but also one filled with contradictions, crooks and bends. There is nothing static about life. No man can step into the same river twice. For the river is not a constant; it is continually moving, and so is life.

When we embark on the road of the journey of life, we travel with trepidation at best, not knowing where the next bend in the road of life will lead. I have resolved to write this book for every one who is interested in the greatest journey ever undertaken by human kind. To every man, there is a high road and a low road. The road to our spiritual Canaan is the high road. Our lives must transcend the low road. The transcendental life walks the high road with the full assurance that that is the road that God walks. Note two things here.

First, the road to Canaan becomes the high road of life because it is on this road that God leads, guides, rules, and dwells. Canaan is God's provision, and the way to it is the way in which God leads. The low road is the road of the misty flats. All those who choose not to travel the road to Canaan become "the rest." The high soul will choose the high road and the low soul will choose the low, and down between the misty flats "the rest" will drift to and fro.

On life's greatest journey, it is impossible to foresee, plan, prepare, or hypothesize exactly what problems we will face next. We are convinced that we do not and cannot know what the next problem will be on this road to Canaan, but we do know who will be there, leading, ruling, and indwelling our spirits.

The bends, crooks, and contradictions on this road to Canaan are inevitable; therefore, certain things must be in place in our lives. In developing and strategizing a plan to successfully navigate the road to our spiritual Canaan, at least one thing must be sure. We must have a right relationship with God. If our relationship with God is in place, difficult situations encountered on the road to Canaan will serve only to reveal the righteousness of God from faith to faith. With this faith we will then be capable to channel out of the boundary, that in which we may be presently confined.

Secondly, being fully cognizant that life's greatest journey is a high road and fraught with obstacles, and for it we need a strategy. A good strategy as we travel the high road is to:

(a) analyze and evaluate our personal experiences;
(b) decipher the messages and the lessons learned from previous experiences of deliverance; and
(c) develop an ability to decipher the theme and motif of the experience and the message it was trying to convey.

You can then attach meaning and purpose to that experience and that will help you to make the right decisions in future situations with which you are confronted. It is crucial to remember that life is full of pre-conceptualized lessons that confine us to the boundary in which we may be stuck.

It is true, make no mistake about it, that you will go through real life experiences. However, the journey of the Canaan odyssey of ancient Israel is a great guide for the greatest journey of your life. It lays down the rules of the road, from which you can derive and gain the knowledge to know how to proceed with a given situation in your journey of life.

The author wished he could draw a map that depicted Israel's sojourn from the shackles of Egypt to the land of milk and honey. Such a map would show the barriers, hindrances, and obstacles that faced Israel. Obvious would be such forces as the Red Sea, the desert, the rivers, and the mountains.

What a map such as this one would not show, however, is the internal journey that went alongside the physical journey. In the journey from Egypt to Canaan, Israel's experiences included much more than their physical travel. They were involved in discoveries—discovery of themselves as a community of God and the awesome responsibility that came with it.

Such a map that does not, in some way, show the inner and deeper journey would be woefully incomplete. The physicality of the journey would be supplemented by the spiritual. Such physicality would include doubting God's love and care, yielding to temptation, and turning away from the divine to a lesser goal. We still face these propensities today on life's greatest journey, the journey of life.

In addition, this book is about a journey–life's greatest journey. We must not see it as a journey we have to make on our own. Others have made this journey before us and left us encouragement and guidance so that we may follow them. We could think of them as having drawn maps based on their life experiences and insights, which we can use to navigate. They developed ways of coping with the tiredness, cynicism, and downright waywardness they knew on their journey. Its milestones are stained with tears and some have passed on their experiences and insights to those who follow.

This journey is also about a journey of faith, and the ways in which we can come close to God before we meet Him face-to-face at the finishing line. In my opinion, this journey of life will be the greatest journey ever undertaken and will bring immense satisfaction and fulfillment to those who have embarked on it. But I admonish you as well: it is difficult, dreary and, in some instances, devastatingly lonely. Those who would dare to travel this road will need constant encouragement and reassurance from those who have undertaken the journey before them.

To begin this journey is to encounter God. To encounter God is to commence a life, a new way of life so radical that we could truthfully say we have been "born again."

This book is about a journey, which for many has already begun. Some have been on this journey since childhood. For them, this book represents a deeper quest into what is already known, yet not fully aware of what it all means. The journey proposed by this book promises to be rewarding. It will illuminate the trails and paths that you may have already traveled, making the next trail and the best path much easier to travel.

The Journey to Canaan

All through the canon of scripture, we are faced with the imagery of a journey. Looming above all of the images of a journey of God's chosen people is the forty-year sojourn of ancient Israel from its slave state of bondage in Egypt to Canaan. We also read of Abraham moving by personal faith to leave his hometown and significant others to seek a place chosen only by God Himself. Abraham did not know where he was going, but he was urged on by unwavering faith in God. In Hebrews Chapter 11:8–10, we read:

> "⁸By faith Abraham, when he was called to go out into a place which he should after receive for an inheritance, obeyed; and he went out, not knowing whither he went. ⁹By faith he sojourned in the land of promise, as in a strange country, dwelling in tabernacles with Isaac and Jacob, the heirs with him of the same promise: ¹⁰For he looked for a city which hath foundations, whose builder and maker is God."

While Abraham did not know where he was going, from the text, we are certain he knew with whom he was traveling, and that mindset sustained him.

Biblical history informs us that many Jews from all over the world made the pilgrimage to Jerusalem. They clearly understood that on their journey there would be mountains to climb and harsh conditions to face, yet they were urged on by the mindset that they had the presence of God as they traveled. Historically, in the first century, Christians were seen as "journeymen and pilgrims."

The text of the New Testament informs us that the terminology used to designate Christians was "those who belong to the way" (Acts 9:2). They were perceived as those traveling on their way to Jerusalem. Developing a mindset of life being a journey through the world offers us a mental picture through which we can visualize the Canaan road. Consider the following postulates:

The image of a journey reminds us that we are going somewhere: we are on our way to Canaan. It encourages us to use this mindset to think ahead and look forward with anticipatory joy of the day when we set foot on the proverbial sacred soil of our Canaan. With this mindset we are assured, if we are faithful and obedient travelers, we shall one day see our Lord face-to-face.

The second mindset is to realize that traveling is not an end in itself. Traveling does more than point us toward the goal of our journeying. It is the process of the journeying that causes us to grow and develop as we move methodically toward our Canaan.

Travel is about finally reaching and achieving our journey's end, with all the joy and gladness appertaining thereto. But it is also about developing personal and spiritual stamina internally as we travel. Therefore traveling on the road to Canaan is a process that catalyzes our development as the people of God who, by faith in His word, persevere and press ever onward.

We must travel this Canaan road with the mindset that we will not be the same people that started out when we reach the finishing line. By the time we reach Canaan, we should be a different people—different because the process has changed us based on our experiences in getting there. This journey to Canaan offers us the chance to deepen our commitment to its object. As we journey, we have the opportunity of reflecting on our goal and anticipating our arrival. The modern New Testament Christian mindset is linked to the philosophy that we must see ourselves as travelers, not settlers. We are constantly moving, marching, changing, evolving, and becoming. We are passing through this world, not adjusting to it in the sense of remaining in it.

This journey to Canaan is long enough to allow us to clearly understand ourselves better. There is a humanistic duplicity about all of us who are people of God. We have strengths and weaknesses, some of which are known and others that are hidden from us. Through our strengths we can better navigate the Canaan road. Through our weaknesses we face delays on the Canaan road.

The God of the Canaan Road

There can be no successful navigation of the Canaan road without a cognitive understanding of the God who is beyond the Rubicon. In the story of Jordan, Joshua calls God, "the living God," and "the God of the whole earth." If he had not been of that ilk, there would not have been any passage of the Jordan under his ministry.

The God of the Canaan road is not only the living God, but He is also the God of the whole earth. Joshua's God was not relegated to a certain locality, as were local deities! He was God even beyond the Rubicon, and on our journey to Canaan we need to know this God. More importantly, we need to know this God fully, not simply know things about Him.

It is a great and noble privilege to know God. It is even nobler to know that God knew us even before we were born. He knows us well enough to know exactly who we are. He knew that some of us would fail Him on our journey because of our personal weaknesses, and others through our human propensity to rebel. There is no pretense or deceit: He sees us as we are and is able to penetrate through the façade that we erected to preserve our public image. He sees all the good as well as the bad that we do. There is no question that our God knows us (Ps. 139:1).

When we internalize that thought, it's enough to cause us to shutter and shake! Just imagine being known, "warts and all" (to use Oliver Cromwell's famous phrase). For some, myself included, this thought can be disconcerting or reassuring. In our worship of prayer, we do not need to pretend about anything. We do not need to live in some make-believe world in which we constantly struggle to live up to the image we have created for ourselves. In prayer, we enter into the caring pretense of one who created us and knows us through and through.

On the Canaan odyssey, we need to establish our relationship with God. This relationship involves our minds, wills and emotions. To know about God is good; it will probably protect us from error and confusion, though it may not succor us any place else. Our wills need to be directed toward God with a new intensity and commitment and done with genuine feelings as well.

On the Canaan road, fellowship is important and crucial with your fellow travelers. What is even more crucial is the presence of the living God! We need to know that He cares, not simply as a theological opinion but as a life-giving and life-sustaining reality upon which the journey to Canaan depends, from beginning to end. Parker makes a salient point in this regard:

> "What matters supremely, therefore, is not in the final analysis, the fact that I know God, but the larger fact, which underlies it—the fact that He knows me. I am graven on the palms of His hands. I am never out of his

> *mind. All my knowledge of Him depends on His sustained initiative in knowing me. I know Him because He first knew me, and continues to know me. He knows me as a friend, one who loves me: and there is no moment when His eyes are off of me, or His attention distracted from me, and no moment, therefore when His care falters."*
>
> —J.L. Parker

These are comforting words, enormously encouraging. They paraphrase and summarize David's psalm. In Psalms 121, we read:

> *"I will lift up my eyes to the hills, where all my help come from? My help comes from the Lord. The maker of heaven and earth. He will not let your feet slip. He who watches over you will not slumber. Indeed, He who watches over Israel will neither slumber nor sleep. The Lord is your shade at your right hand. The sun will not harm you by day, nor the moon by night. The Lord will keep you from all harm. He will watch over your life; The Lord will watch over your coming and going both now and forever."*

Without question, if these words were internalized they would be absolutely comforting to any soul on the Canaan road. The traveler on the Canaan road would naturally be anxious about the danger and hardships he would have to endure, such as climbing steep and rugged hills or coping with a harsh climate. In the midst of these eventualities, we have the words of the Psalms. The psalmist reaffirms the constant, continual care of God throughout the Canaan odyssey. In the knowledge that the living God, who is the God of the whole earth, cares and provides for us, it's comforting to know His constant presence shall sustain us. It is with this faith that we undertake the Canaan road odyssey wherever it takes us!

Chapter 1

Rules
of the
Canaan
Road

"But we will not boast of things without our measure, but according to the measure of the rule which God hath distributed to us, a measure to reach even unto you."   II Cor. 10:13

Chapter I

No man is an island. No man stands alone. From the morning of creation to the dawning of the twenty-first century, man has been subject to rules. In all of human life, human beings are circumscribed by rules. Living without rules is tantamount to playing a game of football or basketball without rules.

Historically, those who accept the biblical creation record believe that man was introduced into this cosmos by a creative act of God. Immediately upon creating Adam, the federal head of the human race, God set in motion a system of divine restraint. In the first book of Moses, Genesis 2:16–17, we read:

> *"¹⁶And the LORD God commanded the man, saying, Of every tree of the garden thou mayest freely eat: ¹⁷But of the tree of the knowledge of good and evil, thou shalt not eat of it: for in the day that thou eatest thereof thou shalt surely die."*

The world is a community, and all living in that community and travelling the road to Canaan must answer for themselves, at least three questions:

1. "Who am I?"—This is the question of identity
2. "How shall I relate?"—This is the question of community
3. "Whom shall I worship?"—This is the question of religion

1. WHO AM I?

There is an unspoken rule of life that demands we know who we are as individuals. "Who am I?" This is the question of identity. It does not matter if one decides to live in a cave, in total isolation; he still must grapple with who he or she is. Shakespeare said, "know thyself;" Aurelius said, "control thyself;" but Jesus the Messianic Master said, "deny thyself." Either way or whichever of these peers you choose to follow, we are still brought into direct confrontation with ourselves. It is a biblical truism that self-identity is foundational.

In that great Sermon on the Mount, Jesus tells His followers to love. Then He tells them, in the final analysis, to love their neighbor as they love themselves. The declarative statement of the Master presupposes a self-awareness of His followers.

We cannot love ourselves in the absence of knowing our own selfhood. A positive selfhood is attainable and demands such awareness for the Canaan road odyssey. Knowing who we are goes to the question of self-satisfaction. To truly know who we are is to be truly satisfied with ourselves. Satisfaction with oneself insulates one from jealousy and envy toward others. If, when we look in the mirror and the image looking back at us is one that we have grown to be completely satisfied with, we then have the beginning of a positive self-concept.

Jesus is the paradigm of all life and the epitome of true selfhood. No man or woman, sinner or saint, can truly know him- or herself who does not first know Jesus. To know oneself is to know Him. If you really want to know who you are, you have to first check with the maker and preserver of all life.

The creation record of Holy Scripture makes known that the God of heaven created man. In Genesis 2:7, we read:

> *"And the LORD God formed man of the dust of the ground, and breathed into his nostrils the breath of life; and man became a living soul."* (Emphasis mine)

To understand the creation of man is to acknowledge that man is a soul, which lives in a body and has a spirit. Man, according to holy writ, is the result of a creative act of Almighty God. The possession of a spirit answers the question: In whose image was man created. God, in the creative act, gave us of His spirit. Accordingly, man is more than a biological creature; he is a spirit being.

Martin Buber said, "There is a certain I-thou concept about the existence of man. 'I' represents the humanity of man, and the 'thou' represents the God conscientiousness within and above man." When there is a synchronicity between the I and the thou in the human existence, man at that juncture becomes whole and complete. He reaches the apex of his human existence, bio-psychosocially and theologically. The prolific Paul clearly spoke to this postulate. In Gal. 2:20, we read:

> *"I am crucified with Christ: nevertheless I live; yet not I, but Christ liveth in me: and the life which I now live in the flesh I live by the faith of the Son of God, who loved me, and gave himself for me."*

Paul not only speaks to the I-thou postulate; he also deals with the essential constituency of man. In I Thess. 5:23, we read:

> *"And the very God of peace sanctify you wholly; and I pray God your whole spirit and soul and body be preserved blameless unto the coming of our Lord Jesus Christ."*

Summarily, "Who Am I?" The divine maker and creator of man has determined that each of us are:

- The result of a creative act of Almighty God
- A soul, living in a body and has a spirit
- A human being and a spirit being
- A trichotomy consisting of a body, a soul, and a spirit
- Complete and whole, when our humanity and our spirituality are synchronous in existence.

To achieve this synchronicity, this wholeness and completeness, you must know Jesus. To know Jesus is not [here] meant to know *about* Jesus, but to *know* Jesus. Through faith you can know Jesus. You can know Him if you believe who He is, what He has done in the atonement, and that He dwells in you upon your completion of obedience to His commands of obedience. We know Him when we believe in Him as the Holy Scripture declares Him. To know Him is to love and follow Him. To the degree that we do this, it will be to that degree that we know who we are and what we were created to be. It is through this faith that we make the I-thou connection.

You are not and do not have to be what others say you are. If you are a disciple of Christ, you are who He says you are. The strongest human drive to achieve should be the drive to be more like Jesus. No other pursuit is higher than the pursuit to know Jesus! Paul addressed that question in one of his prison epistles. In Phil 3:1–10, Paul submits his apostolic dissertation on his selfhood. He recites his credentials when he talks about his I-thou circumstance:

- I am of the stock of Israel, tribe of Benjamin
- A Hebrew of the Hebrews
- As to the Law—a Pharisee

- As to zeal, I persecuted the church of Christ
- As to my morality—blameless
- As to my academic and theological attainments—I count them as loss and dung when compared to the excellency of the knowledge of Christ Jesus.

When asked what is most important in his life, Paul retorts, *"that I may know Him..."! For when I know Him, "I know me."*

Finally, the great and venerable apostle closes his dissertation with these words, and they are very germane to this section. In I Cor. 15:10, we read, *"But by the grace of God I am WHAT I am..."* (Emphasis mine).

It is by the grace of God that we can know who we are. It is by His grace that we can know what we are. Without a true knowledge of the Messianic Master we can do nothing that is lasting.

So, on the road to Canaan, as we live in community, we must make a decision: a decision to know Jesus, or decision to reject Jesus. Life and our human existence afford us that opportunity. We can, however, choose to be nothing, know nothing, do nothing, and die and leave nothing.

Ancient Israel had to make that decision. It was either Egypt or Canaan; it could not be both. Certainly there will be no Canaan unless there is a complete break from Egypt. Chapter II will show the dynamics and ramifications of such a decision as they faced detours, dead ends and dry places on the road to Canaan.

This I-thou concept and its mindset, when fully developed, maturates and reaches into all areas of our personal and social relationships. What another may have will no longer intimidate those who have developed a strong self-concept based on who Jesus was and is. Selfhood is therefore mandatory on the Canaan road. For, in the absence of which, we will be forever frustrated and the demands of the Canaan road will be overwhelming.

2. HOW SHALL I RELATE?

The second question, similar to the first, is one that deals with relationships: "How shall I relate?" If we are going to live in community and walk the Canaan road, we must know how to relate with and to other people! Community demands that we get along with others. This rule is also fundamental and is interlocutory with the former. If the former question is not adequately answered, the second, the one of relationships, will be a living disaster. Rodney King was on point when he postulated the question; "Can we all just get along?" He raised a fundamental question. It was a question of Americanism; it was a question of democracy, yea, even a question of theology. It goes to the question of criminality, delinquency and degeneracy.

The respect for the sacredness and dignity of the human personality depends on our ability or non-ability to answer these basic questions of self-concept and relatedness. Our personal lives will be disruptive and destructive to all others in community when we try to live out our lives with a warped concept of "me-ism"!

In the story of the gospels, we are afforded a paradigm that will assure us of a sure strategy for relating to others in community. Jesus, the master teacher, instructs His disciples how to have and maintain relationships in community. In John 13:23, we read:

> "A new commandment I give unto you, that ye love one another AS I have LOVED YOU." (Emphasis mine)

A cursory look at the cultural history of that bunch of men He had chosen to be His ambassadors of the good news of the gospel reveals many human flaws.

Peter, one of the central figures in the apostolic band, is a case in point. He said to Peter, "…Love others as I have loved you." If Peter had taken an introspective look at himself he would have clearly seen a person with several shortcomings. He was vindictive, hot-headed, partial, foul-mouthed, and a habitual liar. But the cutting edge of the words of the master, "…as I have loved you," was potent and mentally arresting. "…As I have loved you" was designed to get Peter and that small group of disciples to look at themselves. The master said, without saying, "you all had problems, you still have problems, but I love you in spite of your problems!"

When you meet and greet those on your journey that have equal problems, do not ridicule or belittle them or think yourselves better than they. Remember you too had problems, "but I loved you in spite of those weaknesses." This then, is the way you relate to people. Deal with others based on your problematic history and present propensity to fall and make mistakes! Simply put, "do unto others as you would have them do unto you." If we had this mindset, we could be positive forces while on the Canaan road. The apostle Paul addressed this question in his letter to the church at Galatia. In Galatians 6:1, we read:

> "Brethren, if a man be overtaken in a fault, ye which are spiritual, restore such an one in the SPIRIT of meekness; CONSIDERING THYSELF, lest THOU also be tempted." (Emphasis mine)

The love of Jesus in the heart of every Canaan traveler is fundamental and foundational. The love of Jesus was an "agape" love. This love, simply put, says, "I love you, not because of who you are, but because of who I am." With this mindset, we can love any and all persons. This love transcends all racial boundaries. It overlooks political, economic, and social states of deprivation and previous conditions of servitude. This love allows us, with reservations, to reach down to the lowest and up to the highest in community. It is not dependent upon what one can do for you. It's not about who one is, or what one's previous or present status is—it's about "who you are"! This is the philosophy that should guide us as we live and work in community and walk the Canaan road.

3. WHOM SHALL I WORSHIP?

This is the question of religion. All persons are worshipping creatures. All persons will worship something or someone! It's innate. The human family was created with a capacity to worship. In too many instances, our worship has been misguided and misdirected; yet we worship. Whatever we give quality time to, more than anything else, to that degree we are worshipping. Whatever drives you to engage your talents, time and possessions to the exclusion of all else, you are worshipping. One can worship at the altars of materialism, humanism, and modernism, or one can worship God. The ancient people of God were admonished to not forget whom they should worship. In Exodus 20:1–5, we read:

> "...^{3}*Thou shalt have no other gods before me. ^{4}Thou shalt not make unto thee any graven image, or any likeness of any thing that is in heaven above, or that is in the earth beneath, or that is in the water under the earth: ^{5}Thou shalt not bow down thyself to them, nor serve them: for I the LORD thy God am a jealous God, visiting the iniquity of the fathers upon the children unto the third and fourth generation of them that hate me.*"

Jesus, the Christ of God, spoke to this issue in Matt. 4:10, we read:

> *"Then saith Jesus unto him, Get thee hence, Satan: for it is written, Thou shalt worship the Lord thy God, and Him only shalt thou serve."*

Nothing in our lives must supercede our worship to God. God must be first. He cannot be sought second. To seek Him second is to not find Him.

To be a responsible contributor in life one must answer for oneself these three questions: the question of identity, the question of community, and the question of religion. Built into each inquiry is the demand for rules. Rules are inescapable. Those who have accepted the son-ship of our Lord Jesus Christ have a divine imperative to obey the rule of divinity. In Colossians 3:15-16, we read:

> *"And let the peace of God RULE in your hearts..."*
> (Emphasis mine)

The word "rule" translates the Greek word "brabeus," which means "to umpire." Literally it means, "Let God call the game." Let God make the call! In the lives of all saints, God must be allowed to call our game (lifestyle). Not only must He be allowed to call the game, we must accept Him as the rule maker. Verse 16 tells us how He rules: "Let the word of Christ dwell in you richly."

To the extent that the word of Christ dwells in our hearts, it is to that extent that God rules in our hearts and, ultimately, in our lives. A man whose life is void of rules is likened unto a house without walls. Rules, laws, and statutes are the safeguards of freedom and liberty. No one is completely free. One man's freedom ends where another man's freedom begins, and the knowledge of its boundaries resides in a clear understanding of them.

So too is it in the Canaan odyssey of life. In the mindset of the views previously addressed, the following three rules are vitally important:

- Stay in your lane
- Keep your eyes on the road
- Obey the speed limit.

This section gives an exposition of these rules of the Canaan road that we must keep ever before us.

Stay in Your Lane

You will see this postulate enlarged when you get to the chapter on the crossing of the Jordan. But for now, in a cursory way, I want to show the importance of staying in your lane. This postulate goes to the question of self-recognition or self-awareness.

Many of us never come to grip with ourselves. We live our lives as great pretenders. We refuse to admit our weaknesses. One of the greatest disservices we can do to ourselves is to live a life of denial. There will always be something in the bio-psychosocial make-up of all of us that need to be fixed, overcome and conquered. Whatever our weakness, we must admit and seek to quit it. We have tendencies to go out of our way to help others with their human frailties and weaknesses, but allow our weaknesses and frailties to overcome us. Too often, we have become experts in this area of our lives. To not deal aggressively with our own weakness causes us, many times, to become highly critical of others that reflect our weaknesses in their lives. Actually, in these cases, we are really criticizing ourselves, outside ourselves.

Refusal to deal with our own personal weaknesses and acknowledge them to ourselves will cause us to accept responsibilities and positions that we are completely aware, we are not qualified for. Insightful people, who recognize this trait in us, will take advantage of us. They will cater to our pride and vanity. They will promote us, sometimes, to the level of our incompetence as a means of eliminating us or getting rid of us. This process is seen quite often in the corporate world. Being elevated to the level of one's incompetence does not necessarily mean that the person promoted is incompetent, but that the level to which he was promoted renders him incompetent.

Staying in your lane means you should know what you can and cannot do. So rather than accept a position you know absolutely nothing about, it might be well if you would choose to stay where you are (i.e., stay in your lane). Martin L. King, Jr., had a familiar quote:

> *"If you can't be a pine on the top of the hill, be a scrub in the valley, be the best little scrub by the side of the rill, be a bush, if you can't be a tree. If you can't be the moon, be a star. It's not by size you win or fail, be the best of whatever you are."*

Clearly, Dr. King was saying, stay in your lane. He had another quote, which goes to the question of doing your best where you are:

> *"If it fall your lot to sweep streets, sweep streets like Michelangelo carved statues. Sweep streets like Shakespeare wrote poetry. And when the world passes by your dying brier, they will say, here lies a street sweeper that swept his job well."*

To stay in your lane is not enough. We must stay in our lanes and do the absolute best job that life demands. The world has a tendency of respecting and appreciating those who stick to the task and do their jobs well.

One of the greatest poets of our time wrote:

"If you can build a better house, if you can write a better book, or build a better mouse trap; though you make your house in the woods, the world will make a beaten path to your door."

The biblical record punctuates this very same idea of staying in your lane in reference to the Christian's faith. In the story of the great faith warriors of old as recorded in Hebrews 11:4, 5, 7, we read:

"By faith Abel offered unto God a more excellent sacrifice than Cain..."

"By faith Enoch was translated that he should not see death..."

"By faith Noah, being warned of God of things not seen as yet, moved with fear, prepared an ark to the saving of his house..."

Several potent and powerful points emerge from the above text. However, in deference to the question of staying in your lane, and in order to maintain textual continuity, I will postulate three points. Each point is a derivative, and claims its genesis from the virtue called faith. In Heb. 11:8–10, we read: Abel excelled, Enoch escaped, and Noah endured.

A careful scrutiny of the above extrapolation will indicate and clearly demonstrate that there is a glaring commonality between these postulates. The first commonality—they all had faith! The rhema word from the text also demonstrates that you do not have to get out of your lane to be spiritual or physically successful. The text demonstrates further that you do not have to have the same goals as others for your faith to work! Abel stayed in his lane and excelled. He offered "a more excellent sacrifice than Cain." His faith in God allowed him to excel! It provided him everything he needed for what he needed it for.

Enoch, on the other hand, with that same faith, stayed in his lane and escaped! He escaped death. The Bible said, "...he pleased God...." As a result, death did not and could not apply its sting to Enoch. While Abel excelled and Enoch escaped, the text demonstrates that Noah also stayed in his lane. He endured during a time in the history of man when men had become totally corrupted to the end, that their sins stunk in the nostrils of God.

During this decadent, debase and deviant time, the Bible suggests Noah, with that same faith, endured, "...prepared an ark to the saving of his house." Noah stayed in his lane and received what he needed for what he needed it for. Abel did not get in Enoch's lane, nor did Enoch get in Noah's lane. They each stayed in their own lane and each was successful.

Staying in your lane is crucial on this Canaan odyssey. Your faith in God will work for you as it has always worked for saints of God. Be very careful how you seek to desire what others have. Be very careful how you try to take over what others have gained. Their needs may not be your needs. Stay in your lane, stay on course and through biblical faith, God will surely bring it to pass. In Psalm 37:5, we read:

> *"Commit THY way unto the Lord; trust in Him; and HE SHALL BRING IT TO PASS."* (Emphasis mine)

God has already declared his sovereign presence for all that dare take the Canaan odyssey. He will order every step you take down your lane by faith in Christ Jesus. In Psalm 37:23–25, we read:

> *"The steps of a good man are ordered by the Lord: and He delighteth in His way. Though he FALL, he shall not be utterly cast down, for the Lord upholdeth him with His hand."* (Emphasis mine)

I know this to be true. Repeatedly, I have seen God's work when I totally commit my way to Him. I suggest that the reader allow the love of Jesus to fill you and perfume your life in total commitment. The light of that love has shined and illuminated the life of the writer. I am clear on this point: the light is so bright, as it were, and it hurts my eyes.

Stay in your lane; sometimes you will fall, get tired, and want to throw in the towel, but if you would look toward the light, there will be the hand of God. Stay in your lane, that is the first rule of the road on this Canaan odyssey. It is clear that God has provided a sure-footed faith for the slippery times that you will surely experience on the Canaan odyssey.

Keep Your Eyes on the Road

The second rule of the Canaan road is "keep your eyes on the road." The Devil's greatest weapon against Christians is to get them out of spiritual focus. Just as "staying in your lane" is crucially important on the Canaan odyssey, so is keeping your focus. From the dawn of creation, the Devil has been successful in getting the people of God off-center and out-of-focus. He knows the eyes are the windows of the soul. He knows that what the eye focuses on will eventually find its way into the heart. Once it reaches the heart the body will act on it! The Hebrew writer speaks to this question. In the book of Hebrews 12:1–2, we read:

> *"¹Wherefore seeing we also are compassed about with so great a cloud of witnesses, let us lay aside every weight, and the sin which doth so easily beset us, and let us run with patience the race that is SET BEFORE US, ²Looking UNTO JESUS the author and finisher of our faith; who for the joy that was set before him endured the cross, despising the shame, and is set down at the right hand of the throne of God."* (Emphasis mine)

This metaphoric scripture reminds us that Christians are spiritual athletes and that life is a race, and the race is set. The athletic imagery is appropriate. We have our individual lanes in which we must remain and keep our eyes focused on the Lord and the finishing line. In Shakespeare's play *As You Like It*, he writes:

> *"All the world is a stage, and we are merely players; we have our exits and our entrances; and each must play his part in his time."*

We have a duty and a responsibility to keep our eyes on the prize and stay focused in the time that we have to get to the finishing line. Our focus must ever and always be on Jesus.

In the creation record we are afforded an opportunity to see the Devil at work to get the first family out of focus. He accomplished this by beguiling, bamboozling, and bedazzling the mother of all living, Eve. In the book of Genesis 2:16–17, we read:

> "*¹⁶And the LORD God commanded the man, saying, Of every tree of the garden thou mayest freely eat: ¹⁷But of the tree of the knowledge of good and evil, thou shalt not eat of it: for in the day that thou eatest thereof thou shalt surely die."*

In this reading we are afforded a look at the genesis of religion or religious thought. The first religion of God was a "system of divine restrictions."

The reader must not conclude from the above definition of religion that the theology of God is exclusively a system of restrictions. While it is a system of divine restriction, it is certainly more than that. It is redemptive. It is grace. It is law. It is a reign of God. It is all of that, but in the creation record, we get a first look at the religion of God as given to man, and we see a system of divine restrictions. And as we read the text, we see something else. In the same book, chapter three and verses one through six, we read:

> "*¹Now the serpent was more subtil than any beast of the field which the LORD God had made. And he said unto the woman, Yea, hath God said, Ye shall not eat of every tree of the garden? ²And the woman said unto the serpent, We may eat of the fruit of the trees of the garden: ³But of the fruit of the tree which is in the midst of the garden, God hath said, Ye shall not eat of it, neither shall ye touch it, lest ye die. ⁴And the serpent said unto the woman, Ye shall not surely die: ⁵For God doth know that in the day ye eat thereof, then your eyes shall be opened, and ye shall be as gods, knowing good and evil. ⁶And when the woman saw that the tree was good for food, and that it was pleasant to the eyes, and a tree to be desired to make one wise, she took of the fruit thereof, and did eat, and gave also unto her husband with her; and he did eat."*

Rules of the Canaan Road

It is clear after but a cursory look at the text that the devil bamboozled and bedazzled Eve. He succeeded in getting her to focus on herself. Several times he uses the pronoun "you." He says to her "You will not die." Then he says to her, God is actually keeping something "from you." He knows you can become a god and He does not want you to have that knowledge. At this point in the conversation, she loses her focus.

The text says, "…When the woman saw that it was pleasant to the EYES…" she took here eyes off the road, as it were, and had a sin wreck that injured the whole world. We also see "sin" for the first time. We saw "religion" for the first time and defined it as "God's divine restrictions." We see sin for the first time and define it as "breaking through God's divine restrictions."

To disobey God is to break through or go beyond God's divine restrictions. Because of Eve's simple lack of focus in the beginning, we are suffering the consequences of her sin today. Her problem was the taking of her eyes off the road—off God—and placing them on herself! We must not make this mistake on our journey to Canaan. We must not allow the enemy to cause us to lose our focus.

Another case in point that shows the spiritual danger of not keeping your eyes on the road is recorded in Matthew 14:24–31. We read:

> "*²⁴But the ship was now in the midst of the sea, tossed with waves: for the wind was contrary. ²⁵And in the fourth watch of the night Jesus went unto them, walking*

> on the sea. ²⁶And when the disciples saw him walking on the sea, they were troubled, saying, It is a spirit; and they cried out for fear. ²⁷But straightway Jesus spake unto them, saying, Be of good cheer; it is I; be not afraid. ²⁸And Peter answered him and said, Lord, if it be thou, bid me come unto thee on the water. ²⁹And he said, Come. And when Peter was come down out of the ship, he walked on the water, to go to Jesus. ³¹But when he saw the wind boisterous, he was afraid; and beginning to sink, he cried, saying, Lord, save me."

Here is a clear-cut case in point. The mistake that the disciples made in this early episode of this messianic miracle was their failure to internalize the words of the Master. It clearly demonstrates what happens in life when we take our eyes off Jesus; that is to say, take our eyes off the road. When we take our eyes off Jesus and place them on our circumstances, we are heading for trouble. Elsewhere in this volume, I will articulate the need to internalize the words of Christ on our Canaan odyssey.

Jesus had clearly said to them, "It is I, be not afraid." And to Peter, He said, "Come." Peter took his eyes off Jesus and began to notice his surroundings. The consequences were inevitable: "he was afraid; and began to sink." It is not going to matter in this life about our academic, economic or secular achievements; Jesus said, "Without me you can do nothing." Having everything in life is but to have nothing if we do not have a true relationship with Jesus. We must pay attention to Jesus and listen to what He is saying: "be not afraid."

So on your way to somewhere or anywhere, in Jesus, it is fundamental and foundational that we keep *your* eyes on the road, for such is a rule of the Canaan road.

OBEY THE SPEED LIMIT

How often do we get in a hurry and allow the destination to become more important than the process of getting to our destination? On this earthly Canaan odyssey, it is the process that molds us, makes us, and fits us for the destination. Obedience is the key for navigating the process. The process will present what seems like, to us, contradictions and contrary efforts, but the *"counsel of the LORD standeth for ever"* (Ps. 33:11). In the Proverbs 19:21, we read:

> *"There are MANY devices in a man's heart; nevertheless the COUNSEL of the LORD, that shall stand."* (Emphasis mine)

It is important that we understand that the term "counsel" here means "purpose." It is the purpose of God in the process that will ultimately matter. Our responsibility on this Canaan odyssey is to obey. It does not matter how unreasonable the challenges in the process seem, to obey is better than sacrifice. In Isaiah 14:26–27, we read:

> *"²⁶This is the purpose that is purposed upon the whole earth: and this is the hand that is stretched out upon all the nations. ²⁷For the LORD of hosts hath purposed, and who shall disannul it? and his hand is stretched out, and who shall turn it back?"*

There is purpose in the process, just as there is reason for the speed limit imposed on the nation's highways. Our duty is to obey the speed limit. To disobey is to subject us to the wrath of the highway patrol.

A case in point would clearly be the miracle that happened in the fiery furnace of King Nebuchadnezzar of Babylon. In the province, there were three young men by the Hebrew names of Hananiah, Mishael, and Azariah. Their Babylonian designations were Shadrach, Meshach, and Abednego. These young men decided in their hearts that they would obey the speed limit. They were limited to obeying the Hebrew God and none other. In the process of time, kingly orders from Nebuchadnezzar were given to "fall down and worship the golden image, which he had set up."

The story in Daniel 3 suggests that these young men decided to obey God, their Hebrew God, rather than the god of gold set up by the king. Word came to the king's ear that these three Hebrew boys did not go along with the process. These young men knew that they should have no other gods before them, so they chose, rather, to obey God. In the third chapter of the same book, verses fourteen and following, we read:

> *"Nebuchadnezzar spake and said unto them, IS IT TRUE, O Shadrach, Meshach, and Abednego, do not ye serve my gods, nor worship the golden image which I have set up?"* (Emphasis mine)

The king sought to be devilishly accommodating by giving them a second chance to disobey their Hebrew God. In verse fifteen, we read:

> *"¹⁵Now if ye be ready that at what time ye hear the sound of the cornet, flute, harp, sackbut, psaltery, and dulcimer, and all kinds of musick, ye fall down and worship the image which I have made; well: but if ye worship not, ye shall be cast the same hour into the midst of a burning fiery furnace; and who is that God that shall deliver you*

> *out of my hands? ¹⁶Shadrach, Meshach, and Abednego, answered and said to the king, O Nebuchadnezzar, we are not careful to answer thee in this matter. ¹⁷If it be so, OUR GOD WHOM WE SERVE IS ABLE TO DELIVER us from the burning fiery furnace, and he will deliver us out of thine hand, O king. ¹⁸BUT IF NOT, be it known unto thee, O king, that WE WILL NOT SERVE THY GODS, nor worship the golden image which thou hast set up."* (Emphasis mine)

It is clear from the text that these Hebrews said, in effect, "O King, we are not going to argue with you on this matter! We are not going to get caught up in the paralysis of analysis. Our minds are set, and our hearts are determined. We will not bow! We will obey the limits imposed upon us by our God!" This determination created a physical process through which they had to go. In verses nineteen through verse twenty-three, we read:

> *"¹⁹Then was Nebuchadnezzar full of fury, and the form of his visage was changed against Shadrach, Meshach, and Abednego: therefore he spake, and commanded that they should heat the furnace one seven times more than it was wont to be heated. ²⁰And he commanded the most mighty men that were in his army to BIND Shadrach, Meshach, and Abednego, and to cast them into the burning fiery furnace. ²¹Then these men were BOUND in their coats, their hosen, and their hats, and their other garments, and were cast into the midst of the burning fiery furnace. ²²Therefore because the king's commandment was urgent, and the furnace exceeding hot, the flames of the fire slew those men that took up Shadrach, Meshach, and Abednego. ²³And these three men, Shadrach, Meshach, and Abednego, fell DOWN BOUND into the midst of the burning fiery furnace."* (Emphasis mine)

As were Shadrach, Meshach, and Abednego, so must we be on this Canaan odyssey. They said, "we will not bow." To them, to obey and operate within God's divine limits, in the end, would be more advantageous than a quick fix to satisfy some physical propensity.

Having said that, however, to obey the speed limit (operate within the parameter of God's law) sometimes will cause pain and suffering. In a literal sense, to obey the speed limit may or may not get us to where we want to be when we want to be there. It may cause road rage in those who are immediately behind us or those desiring to pass us. Sometimes, as in the case of Shadrach, Meshach, and Abednego, obedience to a higher authority may create a difficult process through which we may have to go, solely because we chose to obey a higher authority.

The lessons from this episode are clearly as follows: (i) God will provide; (ii) God knows the bearing weight of each of our shoulders (note further: they rejected an opportunity to reconsider their position of loyalty to their Hebrew God); (iii) they declared their God was able; and (iv) they submitted to whatever consequences the king would mete out. They resolutely resolved to obey God rather than man, submitted their case to God, and without fear or favor resigned themselves to be thrown into a fiery hell.

This old story of the ancient page demonstrates and firmly suggests how God intervenes when we exhaust our means. Note that these men were "bound" in their own clothing and were cast bound in the burning furnace.

Our Canaan odyssey will abound in personal challenges to our faith and its key will be how we handle ourselves between the time we ask God, and the time God chooses to answer. If we obey and wait patiently, we can have a definite assuredness that, in due time, God will loosen us and answer us. Note further, the Hebrew boys were loosed "in the fire." God did not loose them before going in, nor did He loose them after taking them out. The text says He loosed them "IN the fire!" They were in the struggle and the heat of the fire had already been turned up before God loosed them!

In that distant yesterday, out on a sea called Galilee, the disciples of Jesus were obeying a mandate from the Master: "Let's go over to the other side." Immediately upon embarking on the commissioned sea voyage, a storm broke! Operating within the parameters of the spoken mandates of God does not insure that there will not be unbearable circumstances. But if you remember to obey and do not allow the circumstances to overwhelm you, you will be safe. We have a mandate from God to travel the Canaan road. It is no assurance we will not be bound, 'buked and bruised. But if we stay in our lane and obey the speed limit, God will be with us at each juncture. Stay in the fire! Don't jump out, quit, and withdraw from the journey. Stay in the fire until God loosens you. But He will only loosen you in the fire.

Obey the speed limit. If you get a ticket from a disgruntled satanic road cop, God will meet you in the courtroom, and he has never lost a case. Paul spoke eloquently to this question. He assures all Canaan road travelers that God is faithful and He will provide what we need.

> *"There hath NO TEMPTATION taken you but such as is common to man: but God is faithful, who WILL NOT suffer you to be tempted above that ye are able; BUT*

WILL with the temptation also MAKE A WAY TO ESCAPE, that ye may be able to bear it." I Cor. 10:13
(Emphasis mine)

If you obey the rules of the road, stay in your lane, keep your eyes on the road and obey the speed limit, you will then have yourself in position to meet the challenges of your detours, dead ends and dry places. Each of these elements, as you will see, will be crucial in the crossing of the Jordan.

As you read the rest of these chapters, you will see clearly how important focus will be in determining your success in dealing with the processes of the Canaan road. As Israel, the ancient people of God, had to prepare themselves to leave Egypt, deal with the trauma of the exodus, endure the lowliness of the wilderness, and cross a mighty Jordan, so must we. So must we as God's new Israel. Their journey is a typological and microscopic look at our journey.

If you are going somewhere, if you are going anywhere, the road to Canaan is your anthology. It is clear that no man or woman, sinner or saint, on the road to somewhere, is going to go anywhere worthwhile who disrespects the "Rules of the Road".

Chapter 2

Life's Dilemmas

Detours, Dead Ends and Dry Places

*Developing a Mindset for the
Detours, Dead Ends and Dry Places
on the Road to Canaan*

Chapter II

One must not ever be deceived into expecting life to have uniformity. Life has its peaks and valleys, crooks and bends. A misunderstanding of the seemingly extreme contradictions in life will cause stress, distress, and paranoia.

Down through the arcade of man's civilization, man has tried to define life. In each attempt to define life, each description has been, at most, situational. That is, life is described by each author based purely on his or her personal experience of life.

One author has described life as a voyage, whereupon one sets out on the sea of life, not knowing where the winds of adversity will blow his sails before he reaches the best harbor. Another has described life as a journey, whereupon one strikes out on the road of life not knowing where the next bend in the road will lead. Another has described life as a mountain- climbing experience, where he finds that each rung goes higher and higher.

Martin Luther King, Jr., said, "Even death itself is not a period but a comma in the paragraph of life; it is continuous, it keeps on going." Shakespeare said, "Life is a tale told by an idiot, full of sound and fury, signifying nothing."

In the midst of seeking to understand life, man stands confused and alone. Jesus, the Christ who clearly understands this human frustration, declared, "I have come that you might have life, and that you might have it more abundantly." Life apart from Jesus is frustrating and foreboding. Because of this inability to cope and fully understand life, Canaan sometimes seems impossible. To some, Canaan loses its allure because the price that life

The Journey to Canaan

exacts from us, and its demands made on us, which preoccupies us. We find ourselves exerting major energies trying just to deal with the duplicity and contradictions presented by the process of living. The God of Heaven realized this. He took careful cognizance of it and said to ancient Israel, who was about to embark on its quest for Canaan:

> *"¹When the LORD thy God shall bring thee into the land whither thou goest to possess it, and hath cast out many nations before thee, the Hittites, and the Girgashites, and the Amorites, and the Canaanites, and the Perizzites, and the Hivites, and the Jebusites, seven nations greater and mightier than thou; ²And when the LORD thy God shall deliver them before thee; thou shalt smite them, and utterly destroy them; thou shalt make no covenant with them, nor show mercy unto them: ³Neither shalt thou make marriages with them; thy daughter thou shalt not give unto his son, nor his daughter shalt thou take unto thy son. ⁴ For they will turn away thy son from following me, that they may serve other gods: so will the anger of the LORD be kindled against you, and destroy thee suddenly."* –Deut. 7:1–4   (Emphasis mine)

The people of ancient Israel were located at the last campground in the wilderness, on the plains of Moab, during the interval of forty days before crossing Jordan to begin the conquest of Canaan. As a matter of record, the entire book of Deuteronomy takes place on the plains of Moab. Those who left Egypt had wandered in the wilderness for nearly thirty-eight years and were in the same spot they had been thirty-eight years before. At the beginning of the fortieth year, they were at Kadesh Barnea a second time, and now we have before us the last month in the life of Moses. What was his final charge, his final testament and testimony; what did this great prophet of God have to say to his people? It is what Moses had to say that I want to say to the readers of this volume and fellow travelers to Canaan.

Deuteronomy, the fifth and last book of the Torah, ends on an elegiac note, full of the sadness that all true endings possess. Moses was standing on the peak of Mount Nebo in TransJordan, looking out across the Dead Sea and the river Jordan to Canaan, The Promised Land, that he would never enter. He could see the whole land of promise, from Dan in the north to the Mediterranean Sea in the west to the Negev Desert in the south. Opposite him across the river is Jericho (Moon City , "the city of palms"), according to Deuteronomy the oldest town on earth.

Moses—huge-armed, straight-backed, eagle-eyed—who after so many harrowing meetings with God and disappointments with his people can face death without flinching. We, too, shall die without finishing what we began. Each of us has in our life at least one moment of insight, one Mount Sinai—an uncanny, otherworldly, time-stopping experience that somehow succeeds in breaking through the grimy, boisterous present. The insight that—if we let it—will carry us through our life. However, like Moses or Martin Luther King, Jr., though we may remember that we "have been to the mountaintop," we do not enter the Promised Land, but only glimpse it fleetingly.

Reinhold Niebuhr was correct when he said, "Nothing that is worth doing can be achieved in our lifetime." Therefore, we must be saved by faith and hope. Nothing that is true, beautiful or good makes complete sense in any immediate context of history, so we must be saved by faith in Christ Jesus. Nothing we do, however virtuous, can be accomplished alone; therefore we must be saved by faith, hope, love and obedience of our Lord Jesus Christ!

As I walk through the ancient neighborhood of early Israel, and listen to the pontifications from the pulpit of Moses, I stand in awe. Awe, because I realize that here, in this fifth book of the Pentateuch, I am convinced that Moses is the author of the entirety of the Deuteronomic literature. For it clearly reflects the personality of Moses and the geographical data of Egypt, including the wilderness of Sinai. Yes, the author is Moses, pure and simple. I read where one scribe said, "If the first five books of Moses were not written by Moses, they must have been written by somebody else named Moses." So I stand in awe—awe because Moses rightly gauges not only his time but also our modern times. The "Rules of the Road" given to ancient Isreael, are inndirectly given to us in our trek toward Canaan.

One does not have to be a scholar to discern that "Canaan" could rightly and rightfully represent all spiritual and legitimate secular goals of our modern times. Canaan could very easily represent a certain educational pursuit or goal for the young; a stable marriage for those who seek such; or a career for the career-minded. Canaan is your goal in life. Canaan is heaven where the Messiah has gone to prepare for all those who love Him. Canaan to the sinner might well be the church, the body of Christ, to which one must reach for eternal salvation.

Moses, the great liberator of the Hebrew nation, 1,500 years before Christ, received from God guidelines for deliverance, salvation, success and prosperity. If you, the reader, would adhere to this ancient formula based on divine instructions, you too will be delivered, receive salvation, and enjoy success and prosperity. Moses' assistant minister clearly understood the principle. In Joshua 1:8, we read:

> *"This book of the law shall not depart out of thy mouth; but thou shalt meditate therein day and night, that thou*

mayest observe to do according to all that is written therein: for then thou shalt make thy way prosperous, and then thou shalt have good success."

But God-given success and prosperity are attainable only if the formula is followed and there is strict obedience to the rules of the road. The road to Canaan is not paved and it is not straight. On the road to Canaan the thunder will roll and lightening will flash; you will feel the breakers dashing, trying to conquer your soul. If, in the midst of life's turbulence, you will just be still and fight on, He will never leave you—He will never leave you alone!

On the road to Canaan, let me warn you, there will be detours, dead ends and dry places. However, this three-headed monster is not so intimidating when you know what you have in Christ, and understand Heaven's divine assurance. The psalmist David had that assurance when he penned Ps. 23:1–2:

¹The LORD is my shepherd; I shall not want. ²He maketh me to lie down in green pastures: he LEADETH ME beside the still waters. Ps. 23:1-2 (Emphasis mine)

This is the pivotal thought of the Canaan story: God leads in the ways He wishes us to go!

A Detour Dilemma

"And it came to pass, when Pharaoh had let the people go, that God LED THEM... NOT through the way of the land of the Philistines, although that was near" (Emphasis mine)

God led them. Israel did not determine its route. This must be the mindset throughout the Canaan odyssey. God determines the way we should go. Jeremiah the prophet makes clear that *"It is not in man that walketh to direct his own steps"* (Jer. 10:28). God did not lead them by the direct route because it would have conducted them by way of the Philistine country; the Philistines were strong and would have resisted the invasion by force of arms. Thence, it was that the southern or southeastern route was taken in preference to the northern one. The second stage of the journey was from Succoth to Etham (verse 20). They were just out of Egypt. God felt they were not ready for war. Such an encounter, in the eyes of God, would have motivated them to return to Egypt.

God led Israel on a detour to prevent them from lingering on the borders from which they had just come. Their destination was Canaan. To this effort they must press forward. They must not be allowed to pause on the borders of Egypt no longer than was absolutely necessary! Returning to the former life was too convenient. The pursuer would gain too easy an advantage. There must be no pausing till they were fairly out of the enemy's territory: Succoth to Etham, Etham to Pihohiroth (Ch. 12:2).

In this detour, we see demonstrated the prerogative and sovereignty of God. Commensurately, we must also understand some facts:

- We are blessed on our Canaan odyssey to have the Lord as our guide;
- God's guidance is authoritative; and
- God's guidance is sometimes mysterious.

We see emerging early on in this odyssey, God's divine procedure. We see His turning the Israelites aside from the road, which naturally they would have followed. The way of the Philistines was, no doubt, the road by which they expected to be led. It was the customary road. Geographically, it lay straight before them. It was the shortest and most direct route to Canaan.

Life's Dilemmas

How often does God turn us aside in a detour in providence from what might seem to be the natural course, without a thought to the contrary? He does it even though it may have been the anticipated course of our lives. He led the Israelites by a long detour into the wilderness. Emerging is another dimension of God's procedure. If the end were to escape the Philistines, He did not allow the Israelites room to suppose that He intended to pamper and indulge them. It was clear that where He led them, through the wilderness, was a worse place to travel in than "the way of the land of the Philistines."

In the wilderness, their very faith would be tried and tested. The detour exempted them from warfare with the Philistines at the beginning of their journey, but they still had to fight enemies on the way. Ultimately, God marched them up to the borders of Canaan, to undertake at another point the work of invasion, and the crossing of a dangerous Jordan would precede this invasion!

Even so, it is true in our Christian sojourn to Canaan. The Christian's curriculum is not an easy course of study. Whoever enters upon this Christian journey, expecting to find it all sunshine and roses, is doomed to sorrow disappointments. The road to the Christian Canaan soon takes a turn that leads to the wilderness of trial and testing. The indirect road to our Canaan is not an easy one. It will be fraught with danger, toils, and snares. In so many cases, neither our strength nor our faith will be equal to the opposition we will encounter.

A detour gives us time: time to gather experience, to throw off the habits of servitude, to be brought under subjection, to gain discipline for spiritual war, and to acquire steadiness and courage in facing the enemy. Then again, is this not how we sometimes pray: *"lead us not into temptation"*? (Matt. 6:13) A detour is one way this prayer portion is answered. Our wisdom, under all the circumstances of our lives, is to resign ourselves to God's leading, believing it to be always the best for us. We must make that resolve. The cardinal principle that drives us to that resolution is the fact that God sees what we cannot see. He knows what we do not know. God does not see things the way we see things.

Isaiah said He knows the end from the beginning. Isaiah, the prophet, speaks to the question of the sovereignty and omniscience of God. In Isaiah 46:9–10 we read, *"I am God...declaring the end from the beginning"* and in Isaiah 55:7–9, we read:

> *"⁷Let the wicked forsake his way, and the unrighteous man his thoughts: and let him return unto the LORD, and he will have mercy upon him; and to our God, for he will abundantly pardon. ⁸For my thoughts are not your thoughts, neither are your ways my ways, saith the LORD."*

God never starts anything that He has not already finished. While we may operate under the illusion that the straightest or shortest distance between two points is a straight line, God does not operate under that illusion. If He had, He would have taken ancient Israel through "the way of the land of the Philistines." The Bible says, "It was nearer." Sometimes God has to take us the long way around to get us where He wants us to be! That is why we cannot look at others and determine where we should be in life.

You may be experiencing a DETOUR in your life. If you are young and disadvantaged, you may have had to quit school for a time to help out at home because mom could not do it by herself. You may have had to drop out of college temporarily because of financial reasons. You may have been doing well in school but not well enough to get the scholarship you wanted and needed. Sickness can be a detour. Unemployment, lack of finances, family relationships, personal relationships—all these things and more can cause a detour in your life. But in spite of the detours, we must not give up because we have an assurance that "God is leading!" Even in the detours of our lives, God is leading. His presence is with us! Our task when God is leading is patiently following!

What makes God such a good leader is His knowledge of the end and the beginning. From His vantage point, He sees the entire parade of life. We can only see that portion of life's parade that passes us, but the part we see is not the entire parade. God sees the end from the beginning. He knows our "uprising and our down setting." He knows our hearts, our will, our endurance, our frailties and fallibility. The rest of the text places this power point in perspective:

> **Power Point**
> "...for God said, lest per adventure the people repent when they see war and they return to Egypt."

Sometimes, in our boastful moments, we want others to see us in a different light from that which we really are. We want others to think we are multi-dimensional in talent and skill. We do not want others to know or find out who we really are. We know if they find out who we really are, they would have a different opinion of us. Therefore, we find ourselves living a lie because we refuse to accept who we really are and do our best to make sure no one else finds out. We then, in order to prove the boast, bite off more than we can chew!

How many times have you seen church folks take on responsibilities—enroll in ministries, get on committees—and soon thereafter are no longer attending church. Too much too soon can be dangerous when given to those who are not ready. God sees our heart and knows our shoulders' bearing weight and He allows us to experience detours in our lives.

On the road to Canaan, there will be detours and situations that we may not, and do not, understand. But we have His presence and His assurance that He is leading. Clearly the text expresses three great truisms:

Power Points

1. God is leading.
2. He leads the long way around.
3. He knows the end from the beginning.

We also find in the text another great prerogative of God....

A Deadly Dead End

"But God LED the people...through the way of the wilderness of the Red Sea" (v. 18).

There is a pivotal and central motif in this text that keeps emerging. "God led them." God is still leading, but the text demonstrates that He is leading them to a DEAD END! The Israelites had just experienced a mighty detour in their lives, and then God led them into a dead end. Nothing is more discombobulating than being in a strange part of a town in the dark of night and you find you're staring at a dead end!

So the road to Canaan and our claim on it escalates in trauma. The detour causes wonderment, but it does not adversely affect personal mobility. While we may not understand why God prefers the long way to the nearer way, we are still moving! But the dead end is different. In the dead end, our ability to move forward has been cut off. The way back, over which we have already come, is not the way we wish to return, nor is it an option. But one thing we know for sure: going back will not get us where we want to go, for if it had, we would not be at this point in time and place!

Now add to that the thought that immediately behind you is an enemy with the resources and wherewithal. That enemy will destroy you, your dreams, hopes, and aspirations, and he will soon be catching up to you. The fact that you are also immobilized by an irresistible force that dictates that all you can do is wait for the enemy does not help matters.

Our dead end situation can become so traumatic that, if we are not careful, we will lose sight of His assurance, His presence, and His promise and, inevitably, lose our claim to Canaan! There, in that place, God brought Israel to a dead end to teach them that even there, He is still leading! Israel is now stuck between the sword and the sea, Pharaoh's swords and the Red Sea. This fixation on their own situation causes them to attack Moses verbally. "Why did you not leave us in Egypt?" they cried. They had forgotten their position and were focused in on their condition. God knew, if this nation was going to get to Canaan, at least two things they would have to do to get out of this dead end situation:

1. They must figure out who the protagonists were in the battle for their minds, bodies, and souls at the Red Sea dead end, and

2. They must remember that God is still leading, and can turn desperation into dependence, and sadness into gladness.

This epic battle was between God and Pharaoh. God had to teach Pharaoh a lesson. Israel thought the battle was between themselves and Pharaoh, but not so—it was between God and Pharaoh! The text is clear on this point. God said that Pharaoh, in his heart, would think that this dead end gave him an added advantage over God's people. He would think, God said, "They are entangled in the Land...and the wilderness has shut them in." But God said, "I will harden his heart that he will follow after them; and I will be honored upon Pharaoh, and upon all his host; that the Egyptians may know that I am the Lord" (Ex. 14:1–8). The battle for the minds of men and women today in their struggle toward Canaan is the greatest warfare the world has ever seen and will ever see. It is a battle between sin and evil, right and wrong, God and Satan. In I Samuel 17:47, we read, "for the battle is the Lord's."

On the road to Canaan we will experience dead ends. We will find ourselves in situations where we do not know what to do or which way to go—situations where the clouds in our lives blot out the sun in our lives, situations that only God can fix. It is in these kinds of situations where we have to "be still and see the salvation of God." God sometimes allows these circumstances so we can see Him and know Him better. God created a situation so Abraham would know Him better. Abraham knew God as El Shaddai, but God wanted him to know Him as Jehovah Jireh, so, he commanded him to offer his only son Isaac as a sacrifice.

When, therefore, you find yourself in a "situation," it may be well if you would just stand still, and watch God work! God has a vision, plan, and purpose for our lives. God did not intend for us to work the plan for our lives. He wants us to watch! Watch Him work His plan through us. Stand still when you get to a dead end; call on God and watch Him work!

On the road to Canaan, we need that assurance. Israel had the glorious privilege of watching His work. Forty years He worked miracles in the wilderness. He fed them; He led them. He led them by a cloud by day; He led them by a pillar of fire by night! He is a God who leads! The hymnologist, Edward W. Blandy, who wrote the song *"Where He Leads Me,"* was correct when he wrote:

> "Where He leads me I will follow;
> Where He leads me I will follow,;
> Where He leads me I will follow;
> I'll go with Him, with Him, all the way."

As if life's DETOURS and life's DEAD ENDS were not enough, God continues to show Himself able, adequate and accessible to Israel, and He is still leading!

A Demonstrative Dry Place

> *"So Moses brought Israel from the Red Sea, and they went out into the wilderness of Shur; and they went three days in the wilderness, and found NO WATER."*
> –Ex. 15:22   (Emphasis mine)

God, through His servant Moses, is still leading His people Israel. From a DETOUR to a DEAD END, we come now to a DRY PLACE! On the road to Canaan there will be dry places. How worse can a dry place be than a detour or dead end? All three of these places present similar traumas for the Canaan traveler, but the dry place is the place where there is no water. Where there is no water, there can be no life. Every living organism must have water to survive. There are certain things the human personality needs to properly survive: food, clothing and shelter. But there is another added need; it's called companionship. The author will take the liberty to describe some dry places in life. Following are some suggestions to help you know when you are in a dry place:

- Old friends don't speak to you—you're in a dry place
- Your children forget Mother's Day—you're in a dry place
- The one you love does not love you back—you're in a dry place
- The more you give, the more is expected—you're in a dry place
- You get sick, the sick you visited don't visit you—you're in a dry place
- Loved ones hurt you, but it doesn't hurt any more—you're in a dry place
- You have money, but no one to spend it on—you're in a dry place
- You have a house but the house is not a home—you're in a dry place
- People love you only for what you can do for them—you're in a dry place
- The good you do is totally misunderstood—you're in a dry place
- The children you've raised blame you for their failure—you're in a dry place
- Your friends laugh in your face and stab you in the back—you're in a dry place
- The folks you've helped, help everyone but you—you're in a dry place
- You say "I'm sorry," but sorry is not enough—you're in a dry place

I am convinced, even as I write these words, that some of the readers of these pages could testify, if called upon, to identify some dry places in life. You might say:

- When you lose that which gives meaning and importance to your life—you're in a dry place
- Whenever that one upon whom you were relying no longer satisfies you—you're in a dry place
- Whenever that which previously put a smile on your face and joy in your heart no longer does the trick— you're in a dry place
- Whenever that in which you have invested your life no longer gives the returns you expected— you're in a dry place
- Whenever your bank account no longer provides the interest you once received—you're in a dry place
- Whenever all your assets turn into liabilities— you're in a dry place
- Whenever you come to church Sunday after Sunday and sing songs, but have no song in your heart— you're in a dry place
- When you can go for days and never look at the word of God—you're in a dry place
- When you can go for weeks and never pray or witness to an unsaved soul—you're in a dry place

As you go through life, it is so dangerous to take your water for granted. Your water is a blessing from God. Just because you may not be in a dry place today, does not mean you will not be in a dry place tomorrow.

- God does not have to send the sun everyday, but He does
- God does not have to send us fresh air to breathe every day, but He does
- God does not have to allow us to breathe in and breathe out, but He does
- God does not have to keep our hearts beating every day, but He does

- God does not have to give fertility to the soil and seed in the spring to yield its fruitful harvest in the fall, but He does
- God does not have to send the water of friends, family, health, and length to our lives, but he does

Whatever the water in your life, acknowledge that it is not because you worked for, earned, or deserved it, but it's there because a gracious, merciful, and kind God gives it to you. Just as surely as the Lord brings water to your place, He can take it away. The same God that gives is the same God that takes. We brought nothing into this world, and it is certain we will carry nothing out.

If by chance your place becomes dry, I have a few suggestions. First, don't panic. Many who have seen their places dry up panicked in the process. When the economy takes a downturn and when their future looks bleak, they panic. Some who lose their jobs panic. Some who have suffered devastating personal problems panic. The message this book brings is that God wants us to not panic when we find ourselves in a dry place.

- You can't drown your troubles in a bottle; pills cannot pick up the pieces
- You can't chase away your sorrows by singing the blues
- If Joshua had panicked, the walls of Jericho would never have fallen
- If Caleb had panicked, he never would have said, "Let's go up and possess it"
- If David had panicked, he never would have defeated Goliath
- If Shadrach, Meshach, and Abednego had panicked, they would not have survived the fiery furnace

Life's Dilemmas

- If Paul and Silas had panicked, they would never have had a prayer meeting in the Philippian jail
- If Jesus had panicked, He would never have said, "Father, into thy hands I commend my Spirit," and "It is finished"
- If Jesus had panicked, you and I would still be lost and without God in the world
- If Israel at Jordan had panicked, they would never had gotten to Canaan
- If Moses had panicked, the Red Sea would have never parted

When you panic, you lose control. When you panic, you lose your blessings. Scripture records a list of men of God who panicked and lost their blessing.

- Abel panicked and killed his brother
- Abraham panicked and lied about his wife
- Joseph's brothers panicked and sold him into slavery
- David panicked and killed Uriah
- Moses panicked and broke the tablets of the Law
- Aaron panicked and let the people go into idolatry
- Jeroboam panicked and built two golden calves
- Elijah panicked and ran away from God
- Noah panicked and got drunk
- Lot's wife panicked and looked back
- Saul panicked and spared the life of King Agad
- Peter panicked and denied the Son of God
- The twelve disciples panicked and went into isolation
- The early disciples of Christ panicked and walked no more with Him

When you find yourself in a dry place, detour or dead end, don't panic! Call on God—He hears us. Stand still and watch God work in our lives!

Just remember God is in charge. He is in charge of the water! If you do not believe that the Lord is in charge of the water:

- Ask those disciples on the Galilean Sea: "Was the Lord in charge of the water?"
- Ask Mary! Over in Cana of Galilee: "Was Jesus in charge of the water?"
- Ask Moses! At the Red Sea: "Was the Lord in charge of the water?"
- Ask David! "Is the Lord in charge of the still water?"
- Ask Noah! "Was God in charge of the water?"

On the road to Canaan, one must not allow complacency to set in. The flowing of the water in your life now must not be expected to always be there. Just because you have a bubbling brook today is no indication that will be the case tomorrow. Our Christianity does not insulate us from dry places of bio-psychosocial ills that infect our communities and our world. But we have an assurance that the Messianic Messiah recognized all these social dynamics because He had been through them Himself.

In the Logos chapter of St. John, the Holy Spirit said "He came to His own and His own received Him not." That was a dry place for the Master, so He knows how to handle the dry places in our lives. In Hebrews 13:8, we read: "I will never leave thee nor forsake thee." In John 14:1–2, we read: "I go to prepare a place for you and if I go, I will come again and receive you unto myself."

Again we read in Matt. 28:19–20: "I will be with you always, even unto the end of the world." The reader must be encouraged by the fact that our blessed Lord clearly understood the problems of the dry places, and He is moved by our infirmities and, through His grace and mercy, He brings water into our dry places. As long as God is leading He can, and He will, turn our dry places into fountains, and our fountains into rivers, and our rivers into oceans. He is the God of the dry place just as surely as He is the God of the flooded place.

As we get ready to take our leave from the plain of Moab, getting ready to start towards Canaan, let us remember God is leading! Nobody told Israel the road would be easy. But because He is God, He would not have brought them this far to leave them!

If your life has taken a DETOUR, if you are at a DEAD END, if you are in a DRY PLACE, don't give up, don't give in, and don't give out! The venerable apostle Paul spoke to this question. In Galatians 6, we read,

"Be not weary in well doing, for we will reap if we faint not...."

If you have come through dry places, if you have walked the long way around in the detours of your life, if you have mastered your dead ends in your life, you are blessed! Blessed because at each of these junctures, Christ was leading. You must honor Him and use these instances as motivation to conquer every enemy that will come against you. If you have made it through, you are "more than a conqueror." These places are places where you had an encounter with God.

By encounter, it is meant that at these dead ends, detours and dry places it was the Lord who brought you through. Because of your past deliverance, you know the same God will deliver again! The closer to Canaan you get, the stronger you get, simply because you remember the God that brought you through. You are then assured He will continue to bring you through and lead you safely into Canaan land! Yes, there will be detours, dead ends and dry places in your lives. The Bible says, "They that would live godly in Christ Jesus SHALL suffer persecutions." But we have the assurance of His presence, His promise, and His purpose. As long as you remember what you have in God, remain steadfast; you will reach your Canaan. The venerable apostle Paul addressed this issue in his letter to the Corinthians. In I Corinthians 15:58, we read,

> *"Therefore, my beloved brethren, be ye stedfast, unmoveable, always abounding in the work of the Lord, forasmuch as ye know that your labour is not in vain in the Lord."*

The reader of this chapter, if careful, should have a clear understanding about the crooks and bends, dead ends, detours, and dry places of life and an assurance that there is a lesson to be learned at every crook and bend. However, there is yet another question that begs recognition: "Why must we go through these things? If we are 'good,' why then must we face these travails and troubles?" The next chapter will, hopefully, answer that question.

CHAPTER 3

Why Life's

Detours, Dead Ends and Dry Places?

"…Oh my Lord, IF the LORD be with us, WHY then is all this befallen us? and where be all his miracles which our fathers told us of, saying, Did not the LORD bring us up from Egypt? but now the LORD hath forsaken us, and delivered us into the hands of the Midianites."
Judges 6:13

Chapter III

Why cannot the people of God, having been pardoned of all past sins and having reached deliverance in Jesus Christ, go on to Canaan unabated and unhindered? Why must there be detours, dead ends, and dry places? The reasons are clear. First, man cannot navigate the road to Canaan, independent of God and the hand of God. It was God's desire that ancient Israel would know Him and realize that, on the journey to Canaan, "the battle is the Lord's." Jeremiah, the prophet of God, spoke to this issue in the ancient text when he said:

> "O LORD, I know that the way of man (is) not in himself: (it is) not in man that walketh to direct his steps."
> Jeremiah 10:23 (Emphasis mine)

Secondly, detours, dead ends, and dry places were important in the lives of Israel. God wanted Israel reminded of His sovereignty, and their human tendencies of forgetting His divine sovereignty. There is a tendency inherent in the human personality to soon forget past—and sometimes recent—personal deprivations. God, therefore, led them into situations that presented impossible human extraction. God was intent on showing them that life on the road to Canaan would present situations and scenarios. It would also demand a consciousness of past divine interventions in order to deal with the pregnant present and foreboding future.

God's will was to create in them a clear understanding of the frailty of their humanity and its inadequacy to provide the wherewithal necessary for their personal survival. This power point is clearly seen in the Deuteronomic literature in Chapter 8:1–3; 10–19.

> **Power Point: How to Live**
> *"All the commandments which I command thee this day shall ye observe to do, that ye may live, and multiply, and go in and possess the land which the LORD sware unto your fathers."*
> (Emphasis mine)

The syntax of the text is a creed for abundant living. What clearly emerges is "how to live," which is the first power point. There can be no real or abundant living in the absence of keeping the commands of God. How is the saint of God to live? How is the abundant life lived? A divine snapshot of how the saints of God should live is articulated in the Johanine literature of the synoptic gospels. The great miracle of the Messianic Master, as seen in the graveyard episode in Bethany, is a case in point.

In St. John, Chapter 11, the biblical record and the events surrounding Lazarus' death unfold as paraphrased here.

The sisters of Lazarus had sent a message to Jesus saying, "Lord, behold he whom thou lovest is sick." The message, it seems, was, purposely and deliberately phrased, to apply pressure on the Master: He whom thou lovest is sick! Which is to say, this is not just anybody, this is one that you love, and you should come directly.

It is key to note that the Master had already articulated, "the bird have nests, foxes have holes, but the Son of Man hath no where to lay His head." In other words, the Master had no permanent address! But when the sisters needed Him, the Bible said, "they sent unto Him." That very fact gives consolation to every saint of God. While the Master did not have an earthly address yet, when they needed Him, the Bible said they found Him! Every Bible-believing child of God knows how to find the Lord in time of need.

Their intent wasto get the Master's attention, and have him drop what He may be doing and come directly. But no man can rush the Master or get Him off His schedule. While here on earth He was operating on a divine agenda. He had already told his disciples at Jacob's well (John 4:34):

> *"My MEAT is to DO the will of him that sent me, and to FINISH HIS work."* (Emphasis mine)

When we as saints are living for God, everything else should become secondary, even eating. Living for the Lord demands focus, and Jesus remained ever focused. Having received the message from the sisters, Jesus said, "This sickness is not unto death, but for the GLORY OF GOD." This statement of Jesus answers the question, how do we live as saints of God? The clear answer is, "for the glory of God."

Here was a clear crisis in Lazarus's family but, despite that, Jesus saw an opportunity to glorify God! If we will live for God, we must resolve that even in our crisis, we must find opportunities to glorify God. In sickness or in health, in poverty, or in wealth, our first priority of living is to glorify God. To the degree that we keep His commands, it is to that degree that we glorify God by our living; which ultimately answers the question, "What are we living for?"

That You May Live

God said to Israel in Deut. 8:1–2 *"that ye may live."* To be certain that the concept is biblical, one has but to continue to read the Deuteronomic text:

> *"And thou shalt REMEMBER all the way which the Lord thy God led thee the forty years in the wilderness, to HUMBLE thee, and to PROVE thee, TO KNOW what was in thine heart, whether thou wouldest keep His commandments, or no."* (Emphasis mine)

Previously, I said that God was intent upon creating within the hearts of ancient Israel a consciousness of past and recent divine interventions. Such would allow them to recall the goodness, power and mercies of their God. With this knowledge they could forge ahead in the full realization that the God that delivered them in the past, could be depended upon to deliver them in the pregnant present and the foreboding future. So He said, "Remember. Remember, forty years I led you." The Deuteronomic literature makes that point:

> *"For the Lord thy God hath blessed thee in all thy works of thy hand: He knoweth thy walking through this great wilderness: these FORTY YEARS the LORD thy God hath been with thee: thou hast lacked nothing."* Deut. 2:7
> (Emphasis mine)

> *"Thou raiment waxed not old upon thee, neither did thy foot swell, these FORTY YEARS."* Deut. 8:4
> (Emphasis mine)

This is the human mindset that gives comfort, tranquility, and peace in the time of adversity and stress. This is the sedative that gets you through the darkness between midnight and morning.

God said, "I led you to a detour, a dead end, and a dry place to humble you! I brought you to a fork in the road and took you down a new and unfamiliar path. I took you in a way that was the longer way around. I did not use your concept of 'the shortest distance between two points is a straight line.' I purposely took you the long way around. I took you to a dead end simply to show you that you did not have to worry about fearing Pharaoh, rather obeying me. I took you to an embankment of impossibility, to show you that I can make a way out of no way. I took you into a dry place to show you I could make a fountain out of a rock. Neither of which you could have done yourself. I did it," God said, "to humble you. I needed you to see your inadequacy and realize my ableness. I needed to strip you of your humanistic ego and create within you an abiding dependency on me for and during your periods of desperation. I needed you to see that I am sovereign God and I am God all by myself!"

Now, God said, "remember that and you will live." For it will be to the extent that Israel remembers these experiences that their journey to Canaan will be successful. In Deut 8:10–18, we read:

> *"10When thou hast eaten and art full...11BEWARE that thou forget not the LORD thy God, in not keeping his commandments, and his judgments, and his statutes, which I command thee this day: 12Lest when thou hast eaten and art full, and hast built goodly houses...14THEN thine heart be lifted up, and thou FORGET the LORD thy God, which brought thee forth out of the land of Egypt, from the house of bondage;...17And thou SAY IN THINE HEART, My POWER and the MIGHT of MINE HAND hath gotten me this wealth. 18But thou shalt REMEMBER the LORD thy God: for it is HE that giveth thee power to get wealth, that he may establish HIS covenant."* (Emphasis mine)

That You May Remember

There are several power points in this text. One can easily extrapolate Christian principles from this text germane to loyalty to God. There is a very special power point that emerges in this text that I want to enlarge upon. It goes to the heart of the question: why does God bless us to make money, have jobs, and accumulate wealth?

There are untold thousands of Christians who have lost their psychological and emotional grip on life simply because they fail to heed a simple edict of God's: "Remember." The book of Deuteronomy could well be called "God's book of 'remember.'" This word is pregnant with life and mental healing, ready to give birth; if we would only push! Throughout the Deuteronomic literature God uses the word "remember" over and over again:

> Deut. 5:15, "remember that thou wast a servant..."
> Deut. 8:2, "and thou shalt remember all the ways..."
> Deut. 8:18, "thou shalt remember the Lord thy God..."
> Deut. 9:7, "Remember and forget not how thou..."
> Deut. 9:27, "Remember" thy servants, Abraham, Isaac..."
> Deut. 15:15, "shall remember that thy wast a bondman..."
> Deut. 16:3, "that thou mayest remember the day when thou..."
> Deut. 16:12, "Shall remember that thou was a bondman..."
> Deut. 18:22, "shalt remember...thou was a bondman...
> Deut. 24:9, "remember what the Lord thy God did unto thee..."
> Deut. 25:17, "remember what Amalek did unto thee..."
> Deut. 32:7, "remember the days of old..."

A powerful word—remember. David said, "Bless the Lord O my soul and forget not all His benefits." The divine repetition of the term remember by the mighty God of Israel indicates His assessment of the future. He knows that the only way Israel is going to deal with its present is that it must fully remember its past!

The Deuteronomic scene opens with God giving Israel the key to abundant living. God reminds them of the three impactful things that He performed in the life of Israel as he led it from Egypt's bondage. He reminds them of the detours, dead ends, dry places, and wilderness wanderings. He urges them to recall the past deliverance that He had openly manifested in their lives. Having brought them into direct confrontation with themselves and their recent past, He urges them not to forget. "Do not forget, the Lord thy God in not keeping his commandments." I am, the Lord was saying, the God, not only of today, but also, the God of yesterday and tomorrow. When you begin to prosper, expand, and multiply, and when "thou hast eaten and art full, and hast built goodly houses...then thine heart be lifted up, and thou forget the LORD thou God, which brought thee forth out of the land of Egypt, from the house of bondage.'"

It is certainly not difficult to see divinity in this statement. There is a commonality in the human species that seems to connect us all. There seems to be something innate about the human personality that makes us soon forget those who may have brought us over our mountains of despair, through our valleys and shadows of death! That this is the case, God states in verse 17, and we read:

> "And thou say in thine heart, MY POWER and the MIGHT OF MINE HANDS has gotten ME this wealth." (Emphasis mine)

Spiritual Concept for Acquiring Wealth

God did not want ancient Israel to misunderstand the place of money and wealth in the lives of the people. The misunderstanding of wealth and money has caused millions to lose their vision of Canaan. Some have quit the journey because money and wealth entered their lives! The inspired Holy Book makes clear that "the love of money is the root of all evil." Money is not evil; it is the twisted love that men and women have for it. Money is not inherently good nor it is inherently bad—it is amoral. Money does what one wishes it to do. Money does not make us good or bad. Goodness and evil are virtues or emotions that are driven by human propensities.

The possession of money and wealth tends to make us more of what we already are intrinsically. If one is a drug user, money tends to make him a more active drug user. If one is a moral person, more money tends to expand and enhance that inner morality, which in essence benefits others.

The creator of the universe and the whole human species, knowing this, sets forth a universal principle for all followers of all times. The Deuteronomic scribe sets forth this principle in Chapter 8, verse 18:

> "But (thy) shalt remember the Lord thy God: for it is (He) that giveth thee power to get wealth, that (He) may establish (His) covenant which (He) sware unto thy fathers."
> (Emphasis mine)

The universal principle is clear when this verse is properly exegeted. Assuming the stipulation that the very ability to live, move, and have our very being is purely a divine prerogative and grace favor, let's concentrate on the pronoun "that," in the verse.

The term "that" gives reason and motive for the divine favor bestowed upon the people of God to make money and accumulate wealth. Let's zoom in and get a close-up glimpse into the mindset of God. His expectations are that all those whom he favors be gainfully employed, make money, and accumulate wealth.

As previously stipulated, it is God who gives us the power, ability to work, right exercise of our limbs, and the right reception of our minds. All these things come from God, driven by His grace and mercy. Why? Why does the Lord grant us, directly or indirectly, these human and secular favors? What is the fundamental and foundational purpose of the believers being blessed by God to have a job? The germ of the answer is seen in the relative pronoun "that." Beginning with, "that", we are afforded the answer.

> *"...THAT (He) may ESTABLISH (His) covenant which (He) sware unto thy fathers..."* (Emphasis mine)

The covenant under consideration here is the Abrahamic covenant. God made a covenant with Abraham that reaches into the fabric of the twenty-first century and beyond. References to that covenant is replete in scripture:

> *"...In thee shall ALL families of the earth be blessed"*
> (Gen. 12:2,3)

> *"...I will establish my covenant between me and thee...for an everlasting covenant"* (Gen. 17:6–8)

> *"...And in thy seed shall all the nations of the earth be blessed..."* (Gen. 22:18)

> *"...ye are the children of the prophets, and of the covenant which God made with our fathers, saying unto Abraham, and in thy SEED shall ALL kindreds of the earth be blessed"* (Acts 3:25)
>
> *"...And the scripture, foreseeing that God would justify the heathens through FAITH, preached before the GOSPEL into Abraham, saying, "In thee shall ALL nations be blessed"* (Gal. 3:8)
>
> *"...that the blessing of Abraham might COME on the Gentiles THROUGH JESUS CHRIST, that we might receive the Promise of the Spirit through FAITH"*
> (Gal. 3:14)
>
> *Now to Abraham and his seed was the promise made. He saith not, and to SEEDS, as of many: but as of ONE, and to thy SEED, which is CHRIST."*
> (Emphasis mine)

All the above passages show a scriptural flow of the covenant context to which God referred in the Deuteronomic literature. In the mind of God we are privileged to see His intent. From the loins of Abraham and his seed would come justification and sanctification of the Gentiles. This all would come in the redemption act of Jesus Christ on Calvary, the seed of the covenant who was to come to bless all nations. We, having received the covenant, which is the gospel, are his covenant people. This gospel must be established in the entire world. Jesus decreed this in the synoptic gospel after His resurrection. He further emphasized the preaching and teaching of the covenant of faith just before He returned to glory. The gospel is the covenant of faith and all who accept it will become covenant children of Abraham.

Clearly, then, the reason that God blesses us with the power to get wealth is to see to it that the local congregation of believers would have the wherewithal to spread the gospel, which is His covenant with believers today. God would have all Canaan travelers today to understand His classical purpose for blessing His people financially. He also desires that from the classical, we extrapolate the modern intent as well.

The primary purpose of our jobs and gainful employment, making money, and accumulating wealth is not to pay personal bills that we may or may not have judicially made. The primary reason the believer in Christ works is to first make sure the "covenant" of God is established in our Jerusalems, our Judeas, our Samarias, and unto the outermost parts of the earth. If this scriptural model were followed, believers would not only be able to purchase airtime, but the television stations and other media outlets.

For those who would say that the paradigm described is Old Testament, I offer almost the exact concept from the mouth of the Messianic Master:

> *"But seek ye FIRST the kingdom of God, and His righteousness; and all these THINGS shall be ADDED unto you."* Matt. 6:33 (Emphasis mine)

Fortification for Detours, Dead Ends and Dry Places

To the degree that the Deuteronomic principle and the principle articulated by Matthew are studiously followed, it will be to that degree that we will have less or more detours, dead ends, and dry places in our lives. This concept, as described by the author, should not be misconstrued as the only concept, and if kept, all else will not be necessary. Rather, this principle gives the believer a better understanding of why giving as we prosper is crucially necessary. How much we give is tied to how much we love Jesus. The determining factors under consideration should be what has He done, what is He doing, and what will He do in the future for all who will dare to keep His commandments.

While God blesses us on the road to Canaan, He expects that we realize the source of our blessings. However, if we choose to forget and not remember, this guarantees we will never claim our Canaan.

Lest I make the mistake of ending this chapter here and not giving the reader a biblical model, strategy, or methodology, I hasten to do so. The Deuteronomic literature in Chapter Eight brings us into direct confrontation with the will of God for our lives; that we remember His mercy and grace, and apply it at every level of our lives. To not do so will dishonor God and His sovereign power, and in turn renders us helpless, hopeless, and hapless when faced by detours, dead ends, and dry places. How does a Christian fortify himself or herself for the inevitability of the dead ends, detours, and dry places that will surely come into the Christian's life in search of Canaan?

Christian fortification is a process that begins at our spiritual birth (conversion). If it does not begin at birth, the satanic influence will become so total and entrenched that spiritual expulsion will undoubtedly become most difficult. It is to this concept that Jesus spoke in Matthew 12:43–45. We read:

> *"⁴³When the unclean spirit is gone out of a man, he walketh through dry places, seeking rest, and findeth none. ⁴⁴Then he saith, I will return into my house from whence I came out; and when he is come, he findeth (it)*

empty, swept, and garnished. ⁴⁵Then goeth he, and taketh with himself seven other spirits more wicked than himself, and they enter in and dwell there: and the last (state) of that man is worse than the first. Even so shall it be also unto this wicked generation."

At spiritual birth, having repented of a sinful past life, we boldly embark on the Canaan odyssey. Having resolved to give up secular sinfulness, having expunged the rooms of sin in our life, we then have a new house. To the degree that we have said no to the flesh, it is to that degree that our house has been swept clean. But new furnishings and new residents must replace the old furnishings and sinful residents. To this concept, Jesus spoke again. In the synoptic gospel of John 14:23, we read:

"Jesus answered and said unto him, If a man love me, he will keep my words: and my Father will love him, and we will come unto him, and make our abode with him."
(Emphasis mine)

Heaven, as it were, comes down to the new convert to set up "residency" in the house that has been swept clean. The Lord does not want our house to remain unoccupied. Therefore, immediately upon conversion, residents from glory come to live (dwell) with the newly converted Christian. At the conversion birth, the newly converted Christian must be taught to allow the heavenly residents to come into their lives and fill the void left by the previous residents. He should not resist the heavenly tenants from having ascendancy in our lives.

Now, how is that done? The venerable apostle Paul has a ready answer. In his letter to the church at Colossi, Colossians 3:15–17, we read:

> *"And let the PEACE of God RULE in your hearts, to the which also ye are called in one body; and be ye thankful."*
> (Emphasis mine)

Here, the paradigm is clear. This is how we fortify ourselves, in addition to what we said in Chapter I relative to the fact of "God is leading." Paul uses the word "let." Let is a present imperative, a command. As Gardner Taylor says, "not to be argued with." It is imperative, fundamentally important and foundational that the Christian, in his basic training, understand that the peace of God must rule in his life.

Much could be said here about the "peace" that Jesus left with His disciples. In deference to that point, I will simply articulate the different ways Paul uses this term "peace." He refers to it as the peace (of) God, peace (from) God, and peace (with) God. Each expression represents a different aspect of the same peace. In the text under consideration, however, Paul says, "let the peace (of) God rule in your heart." Aside from the fact that this admonition is imperative, it also takes on an athletic connotation. That connotation is seen in the word rule. This word has the idea of an umpire. The original word is "brabeuo". The umpire calls the game. He calls the ball and strikes.

At conversion, God becomes the umpire of our lives. Our loyalty then is no longer to Satan; it is to God. He and He alone settle disputes, contradictions, rights and wrongs that may surface in our lives. This is the method that Christians must use in their marriages and social relationships. This is also the method congregations must use in settling disputes, conflicts, and disagreements. Let God rule; let God umpire and let Him call the shots! This is the first strategy of Christian living. Let God rule! There is only one umpire on the Canaan road. He is our God and He rules!

Secondly, Paul says in verse 16, and we read: "Let the words of Christ dwell in you richly."

> **Power Points**
> v. 15—Let the word rule
> v. 16—Let God dwell

This is how God maintains His rule. This is how the new residents from Heaven rule: through the word. If the word does not dwell, God does not rule. The word dwell, like rule, is pregnant with spiritual meaning. It means to settle down, to be at home, or to have a free range. When visiting a friend's home, the words, "make yourself at home" give you a sense of freedom and comfort, and dispel uneasiness. God rules uninhibitedly in our lives with the word dwell and is at home in our lives. That is the concept and strategy for dealing with detours, dead ends, and dry places in our lives. When we accept this biblical concept by faith and internalize it in our lives, we know that we will be able to walk even through the valleys and shadows of death.

Heart Matters

Finally, in dealing with our detours, dead ends, and dry places, one other point is germane to our discussion. Paul says in verse 15, "...In your hearts...." In verse 16 he says, "dwell in you...." The word "you" has the word "heart" as its antecedent. The peace of God must "rule" in our hearts, and the word must "dwell" where the ruling is done. This all takes place in the "heart." Why in the heart? The heart, as used here, means the mind of man. It is here, in the mind, that the battle of life is fought.

The greatest battle of history is not the battle of World War I, World War II, Korea, Vietnam, or The Gulf War; the greatest war of any century of mankind is the battle or war for the minds of men. Paul knew this. Of the numerous times he referred to the minds of Christians, one stands out. In his letter to the church of Philippi, we read:

> *"Let this mind be in you, which was also in Christ Jesus.*
> (Phil. 2:5)

This is where the Spirit of God dwells by faith, in our hearts and minds. This is where the Christian battle is fought. If Satan can capture our minds, we will be unable to deal with our dead ends, detours, and dry places. If he can capture our minds, the Christian, sovereign God cannot rule. If he captures our minds the "words of Christ" cannot dwell effectively. The task therefore, for the Christian today, as I see it, is preserving the mind for the rule of God and the indwelling of the word. The ancient people of God (Israel) were given a strategy and methodology for the preservation (guarding) of the mind for the rulership of God. In Proverbs 4:20–22, we read:

> *"^{20}My son, attend to my words; incline thine EAR unto my sayings. ^{21}Let them not depart from thine EYES; keep them in the midst of thine HEART. ^{22}For they are LIFE unto those that find them, and health to all their flesh."*
> (Emphasis mine)

Herein lies Israel's strategy for guarding the mind. First, God said to them, "attend to my words." From these first words we learn something about God. He wants His people to keep His word. Down through the arcade of man's civilization and in his quest to be acceptable to his God, he notices that the Divine being demands a solemn keeping of His word.

Throughout the Deuteronomic literature, as I have shown in the previous chapter, God constantly reminds Israel to remember His given words. It is by His words we are saved, redeemed, and sanctified. God's words are sufficient to successfully navigate us through the pitfalls, obstacles, and adversities of our earthly life. Jesus reminds us in John 6:63:

> *"It is the spirit that quickeneth; the flesh profiteth nothing: the words that I speak unto you, they are spirit, and they are life."*

Jesus reminds us again in John 12:48:

> *"He that rejecteth me, and receiveth not my words, hath one that judgeth him: the word that I have spoken, the same shall judge him in the last day."*

The imperative "attend to my words" is a universal imperative. For all those who are in a covenant relationship with God, whether under the Mosaic, Old Testament covenant, or the Christian, New Testament covenant, attending to the divine word is universally demanded. The Proverbs text goes to the question of hearing the word. The universality and the validity of these proverbs are seen in the words used by Paul in Romans 10:17. In this verse we read:

> *"So then faith COMETH by HEARING, and hearing by THE WORD of God."* (Emphasis mine)

There are several power points in this verse, but two are crucial for Canaan road travelers. The first is faith cometh. Obviously, our faith is necessary, but beyond that, Paul tells how it comes. The fact that he said faith comes suggests a process—a conduit. How does our faith come? Make no mistake: it comes by hearing the word. We need to be mindful here, for it is here we have missed some pivotal teaching.

Untold gospel preachers and saints of God have quoted this verse and missed the essence of the syntax. Note first what he did not say. He did say our faith comes after having heard. He was clear: faith cometh by hearing. Hearing is a present participle denoting continuous action. So we learn that faith is a continuous inward and outward flow. Our faith is increased at each hearing of the word. While one may have heard a sermon once, that does not mean it should not be heard again! Each time life offers an opportunity to hear the word rightly divided, we should make ourselves available, because that is the way faith comes—by hearing.

The more one hears the word, the more one's faith should increase. Paul then says, "...and hearing by the word of God." Our faith is increased, not by singing or the syncopation of the singing beat, but by the hearing of the word.

Modern day saints on the Canaan road have substituted rhythm and musical syncopation for the preaching of the word. Verbalizing so-called praise and energetic physicality have taken the place of the hunger and thirst for the word, through which our faith in God comes and is increased. So Paul, like the Proverbs writer of old, says to us: "attend to the word."

Having said that, the question that is just as essential and germane is, "Why attendance to the word?" For that answer, we continue with the words of the Proverbs, "Incline thine ear unto my sayings." Incline—lean into the flow of the message. Have you seen people who were trying desperately to either hear or be sure that they heard, lean their bodies so the ears will not miss what the mouth is saying?

People lean in or toward the flow of the message because they have perceived that the message is too important to miss. In the Proverbs text, the word incline gives power and potency to the message that is unfolding. Nothing is more important to a believer than a word from the Lord.

The serious worshippers do not want to be distracted when the word is being unfolded, presented, posited, and preached. Every believer ought to be inclined during worship, particularly during preaching. It is through preaching, according to Paul, that God has chosen to save the world. Not through religious entertainment, but, preaching! He said in the Roman letter, "How shall they HEAR, without a preacher." This is the process and the conduit through which our faith comes! God was very emphatic to ancient Israel about the seriousness of hearing, inclining their ears and focusing on His commands. In Eccl. 5:1, the preacher said, and we read:

"Keep thy foot when thou goest to the house of God, and be more ready to HEAR, than to give the sacrifice of fools." (Emphasis mine)

From ancient times, there has been a definite seriousness about what is heard in the house of God. The writer of the Proverbs elongates his admonition by saying, "Let them not depart from thy eyes." My reference to this text is obvious. A few pages back, I postulated the position that if the Devil can capture our minds, he will render us unable to deal with our detours, dead ends, and dry places. It is for that very reason we must guard our minds.

The Proverb text teaches us to: (i) attend to the word; (ii) incline our ear; (iii) let them not depart from thine eyes; (iv) keep them in the midst of thine heart; and (v) let them not depart from thine eyes. In a word, the text is saying, keep your eyes on the book or, as Jesus did when He entered the synagogue of the Jews, "When He had opened the book, He found the place..." A valuable lesson you learn here is to keep the word in your focus.

What the writer of the book of Proverbs revealed to us, psychologists and psychiatrists have admitted to be true today. The ears and eyes are the windows of the soul, heart, and mind. What gets in through these windows goes directly to the mind.

Freud, in his psychoanalysis of the human mind, sought to enlarge upon this Old Testament scripture. Freud said the mind consists of "ego, id, and superego." Freud took the position that in every man, there is a built-in impressionable mind.

Theologically, the id represents the body, the flesh and all its desires, all it's fleshly propensities. The ego represents the soul. It is in the soul realm that man communicates with man. In the soul lies all of man's emotions. The super ego represents the highest aspect of the constituency of the human species. The Bible refers, in some instances, to the mind and spirit as the same entity. The mind is seen as the standard of man. It is with the mind that we understand how he relates and how he handles the affairs of life that come his way.

What the mind does not do depends entirely upon what it perceives and receives from the external world through the windows of the mind, (eyes, and ears). The Devil knows this, and Jesus knew this. In Matthew 13:19, we read:

> *"When ANY ONE HEARETH the word of the kingdom, and understandeth it not, THEN cometh the wicked one, and CATCHETH AWAY that which was sown in his HEART."* (Emphasis mine)

The Devil knows that God rules where the word dwells. The battle is between God and the Devil, and we are the instruments whom either God or the Devil will use. God's will is that we guard our hearts by inclining our ears to the word and meditating daily in the word. The Devil's attempt to defeat the rule and the indwelling of the word by, "catcheth away that which was sown in our hearts." Jesus compounds the Christian's concept of guarding the heart. In Matthew 13:16, we read:

> *"But blessed are your EYES, for they SEE: and your EARS, for they HEAR."* (Emphasis mine)

Truly, these are the windows of the soul. Ancient Israel heard the words of Jehovah. Israel saw the wondrous works of Jehovah for forty years in the wilderness. Moses delivered to Israel the word from God even before it began its historical march toward Canaan:

> *⁴Ye have SEEN what I DID unto the Egyptians, and how I bare you on eagles' wings, and brought you unto myself. ⁵Now therefore, if ye will obey my VOICE indeed, and keep my covenant, THEN ye shall be a peculiar treasure unto me above all people: for all the earth is mine."* Ex. 19:4,5 (Emphasis mine)

It is clear therefore, that God allows detours, dead ends, and dry places that He may humble, teach, and fortify us. He uses the windows of our soul to reach our minds. He says, in no uncertain terms, remember what you see, remember what you hear, as I bring you through your dead ends, detours, and dry places! Why detours, dead ends, and dry places? They serve to make us ever mindful of God's deliverance and grace. They are the catalysts that reveal God's grace in us, towards us, and His love for us.

Finally, and if nothing else, for therein (i.e., in the detours, dead ends, and dry places of our Christian life), is the righteousness of God revealed from faith to faith (from faith, in order to produce faith). Thus the triplets of our trials and tribulations are actually faith boosters, designed in purpose and intent to produce faith ever more.

While the above is true and scripturally correct, our faith works in us and for us. We go through a time of testing that we might receive strength for the next hurdle of life presented to us on our Canaan odyssey. We do not know what we can do until we do it. We could not do it until we did it. When we did it, we then knew we could do it.

We may not have known embarking on the Canaan road would present challenges that would stretch our faith to the limit. We will meet challenges when we initially embark, and we will not know whether we can handle them or not. But we are assured that if we get in the fight, if we get in the fire and stay in the fire until God loosens us in the fire, we will then have the assurance. When we come through the challenge, we come out not defeated, timid, or filled with trepidation, we come out as tour guides: prepared and qualified to lead others through the same experience. Our message of encouragement to them will be simple: "run with patience the race set before you, looking to Jesus."

But each traveler must be mindful that there are "rules" that must be followed. Every traveler on the road to spiritual Canaan has been made free in Christ, but the journey is not over—challenges still lie ahead. In the case of ancient Israel, they have yet another challenge. They are about to face a river more formidable than the Red Sea. To meet this challenge they had to formally prepare themselves.

The next chapter will show how their theology and religiosity had to change to meet that challenge.

Chapter 4

Jordan River

A precursor to canaan

"Forty years Israel ate manna in the wilderness. Manna was desert food, sufficient for desert wandering. But manna will not suffice for the swelling of the Jordan. The diet must change!"

Chapter IV

When we get to Chapter Three of the book of Joshua, we are introduced to character-building concepts that are foundational for the Canaan road mindset. It shall be the intent of the author to do an exposition of Chapter Three, extracting therefrom principles and guidelines for crossing Jordans in your life. Replete in this chapter are instructions, whether we take the words in their natural or literal sense, figurative or allegorical sense. The instructions emerging from this chapter are so multifaceted that it is impossible to theologically package them into three points and a poem.

The time of waiting, in the preacher's case (Joshua), was over. The spies had brought back their report, the way was open, the command clear. The very next morning, and early that night, preparations were made for the decisive step which would commit Israel, the ancient people of God, to the struggle that lay ahead in their possession of the land of Canaan. Clearly, this says when the path of duty is clear, the plan is designed, we are obligated to enter upon the task at once.

There can be no successful crossing of our Jordans without faith. We are afforded a look at obedient faith in the behavior of ancient Israel. They implicitly obeyed Joshua's command, nonsensical as it may have seemed at the time. Jordan was overflowed; the ordinary fords were impossible; there was no way through the river! But cross it, they must! They had been told that "within three days they should cross Jordan and there was neither murmuring or disputing."

The greatest hindrance to spiritual growth is the Christian's lack of faith. Our Jordans, socially, theologically, and familiarly, can be removed by steadfast faith. When we come to a clear understanding of what God requires, we must—as far as humanly possible—be about the business of performing the task. When all the elasticity has been used up in the religiosity of our Christian will, we must then depend on God!

When we place our trust and faith in God, we will find that the same God that transported Israel across chilly Jordan will certainly do the same for us. He can roll back the waves of the Jordan of our life and can arrest the overflowing wickedness of our nation. He can make a way out of no way. He is the only God I know that can hit a straight lick with a crooked stick. He is the only God I know that can stand flat-footed and tiptoe at the same time! He is a God "whose way is in the sea, and His path in the great waters." He is God all by Himself, and will roll all burdens of His people away.

The Preacher–Prophet and His Purpose as Provocateur

As ancient Israel prepares to cross Jordan, we get instructions pertaining to the ancient preacher, Joshua. There is a clear rhema word here about him. First, he must not just be a preacher, but according to this text a leader, provoker, motivator, and provocateur as well.

Let it be said, if the preachers or ministers in the Church of Christ do not resolve to be guides and leaders, the Church is better off without them. If a preacher hangs out his shingle indicating that he is a preacher, he must resolve certain things. He must:

1. prove all things, examine all claims;
2. hold fast to sound words and doctrine;
3. be ready to give an answer of the reason of the hope that is within him;
4. be set for the defense of the Gospel;
5. not be ashamed of the gospel of Jesus Christ;
6. study to show himself approved unto God;
7. be ready to set things in order; and
8. live an exemplary life in Christ. It is idle to preach if we do not practice.

In all things that become Christian, the Christian minister must set the example! He must have zeal for the Master's cause and unwearied efforts to promote said cause. He should also set the example in purity of life—acts of love to the sick and aged, to the young and tender, and in kindness to all. He should be an example in public spirit, moreover, and show regard for the general welfare, in honor, truth, prudence, self-command, and self-abnegation. In a word, the preacher/minister of God should be in the forefront of the grand congregational army, leading and guiding on the way to Canaan land.

Having said that, it is needful to also say a word to the standing army of followers. The congregational army must not follow the aforementioned minister and leaders without a high ideal for the members. It is not sufficient to only lay down a high ideal for our preachers/ministers. Consider the role of the army privates—which is to criticize sharply and closely monitor the actions of those who are charged to lead. Joshua bids the Israelites "sanctify yourselves," because God was about to do a new thing!

As we stand at our Jordans surveying the land beyond, be it secular or spiritual, we must prepare ourselves by prayer and meditation, and by listening to the word of the Lord. God's spirit and presence are ever near us, but at special times He requires that He be specially sought. And he who never permits himself a moment's retirement from the ordinary business and amusements of life may well doubt whether God's spirit has a hold on his soul. We must, like Israel, follow God across the Jordan. God had clearly demonstrated his deity in providing for them for forty years in the wilderness. Next He would demonstrate that they do not go in their own strength, but in His strength.

The question for God's standing army is clear. At what level are we prepared to meet God? He is seeking those who would commit to Him. Are we willing to sanctify and consecrate ourselves and follow Him wherever He may lead? The resolution to do this must not wait. To this end the preacher kept on preaching!

GOD'S CHALLENGE TO THE PREACHER–PROPHET PROVOCATEUR

While we stand here with Israel at the Jordan, let us listen carefully. If you do, you will hear the instructions God has for Joshua, the preacher-prophet provocateur. He instructs him how to claim Canaan. This section is written to help you understand what is involved in making the transitional shift from a defeated wilderness wanderer to living in the land of victory. There are four distinct calls:

- The Call to Claim the Land
- The Call to Have Confidence in the Lord
- The Call to Carry Out the Law
- The Call to Courage in Leadership

The Call to Claim the Land—Joshua, the provocative preacher, is reminded that God has already given the land of Canaan to the children of Israel. He is commanded to lead the people into Canaan to claim the land that they had been promised by the Lord. The land was given to Israel back in Gen. 12:7, and the promises were reaffirmed to every succeeding generation of the nation of Israel. The land was indeed their land. There was no need for them to continue wandering around in the wilderness. They had a land. All that was necessary was for them to claim it.

Those of us who have embarked on the Canaan road must internalize by faith what has been given to us by faith in Christ Jesus. This thought is enlarged in the chapter on possessing your possession. There is no need for Christians to feel or act defeated. If the Christian believes in Jesus, he or she cannot be defeated. In Isa. 54:17, we read,

> *"No weapon that is formed against thee shall prosper."*

Christians who do not take seriously the words of the Holy Spirit will find themselves wandering around in a spiritual wilderness. It does not have to be that way. God has a place of victorious living, which He has promised to all those that love and obey Him (II Cor. 2:14; Rom. 8:37; I Cor. 15:57). If we would only claim through faith all that we have in Christ Jesus, we can walk in righteousness and victory.

The call to the preacher-prophet provocateur was clear. In Joshua 1:2–4, we read:

> *"²Moses my servant is dead; now therefore arise, go over this Jordan, thou, and all this people, unto the land which I do give to them, even to the children of Israel. ³Every place that the sole of your foot shall tread upon, that have I given unto you, as I said unto Moses. ⁴From the wilderness and this Lebanon even unto the great river, the river Euphrates, all the land of the Hittites, and unto the great sea toward the going down of the sun, shall be your coast."*

This word, this call to Joshua to claim the land, comes directly from God. The preacher must take this word to the people. Joshua had a mandate from God, which he had no alternative but to do and say exactly what God had commanded. There is a decisive difference in taking a word to God from the people and taking a word from God to the people. When the word originates with the people, it could well be mixed with selfish motives and human complaints. But when the word originates with God and comes from God to the people, there is no wiggle room! Every word of God is pure! In Prov. 30:5, we read:

> "⁵*Every word of God is pure: he is a shield unto them that put their trust in him.* ⁶*Add thou not unto his words, lest he reprove thee, and thou be found a liar.*"

It seems that this is what Paul had in mind when he spoke to the Romans. In Rom. 1:15, we read:

> "*So, as much as in me is, I am ready to preach the gospel TO you that are at Rome also.*" (Emphasis mine)

It is clear, at times the preacher-prophet must go to God on behalf of the people. But to go to the people on behalf of God is to leave no margin for error in the testimony. The crossing of the Jordan depends directly upon whether the preacher-prophet can get this testimony straight!

The Call to Have Confidence in the Lord—Secondly, the preacher is reminded of some very precious promises in these verses (vv. 5–6, 9). Take notice what God promised him:

1. v.5—The promise of victory over every enemy
2. v.5—The promise of the presence and power of God
3. v.5—The promise of the faithfulness of God

4. v.6—The promise of absolute victory
5. v.6—The promise of God to keep His promises

What did Joshua, the preacher, have to do to make these things happen? Just one thing: trust God! God was going to give Israel the victory. Joshua was merely the instrument that God had chosen to use to do it. These things were going to happen and, for Joshua to be a part of it, all he had to do was have faith in God! God had long ago covenanted to bring Israel into Canaan, the land of Abraham their father. Therefore, Jordan was a non-factor to God. If the preacher would trust God and translate that trust to the people, Canaan would be assured. The key then and the key now for crossing Jordans in your life is, trust in God, in spite of how things look!

We can rest assured that the same promises God made to Joshua are available to all of us today. You can still count on the Lord to do everything He promised Joshua He would do:

1. He still gives victory over all our enemies—I John 5:4,5
2. He is still ever-present—Heb. 13:5
3. He is still all-powerful—Matt. 28:18
4. He is still faithful—Matt. 28:20
5. He still gives absolute victory—I Cor. 15:57; Deut. 21:4, 27
6. He still keeps His promises—Rom. 4:21

What do we have to do today to have these things come to pass in our lives? Just one thing: trust God! As soon as we learn to internalize our faith in God at all levels, we will then walk in righteousness and victory (Heb. 11:6, Rom. 14:23). When everything else fails, faith will ever stand the test! We may let the Lord down, but He will never fail the believer who has his or her faith in Him! David, the great psalmist of Israel, spoke to that question in scripture. In Psalms 118:8, we read:

> "It is better to trust in the LORD than to put confidence in man."

John, the beloved disciple lent his wisdom to this issue as well. In I John 5:14, we read:

> "And this is the confidence that we have in him, that, if we ask any thing according to his will, he heareth us."

The Call to Carry Out the Law—Thirdly, the Lord tells the preacher-prophet that if he is to lead the people of God to rest in Canaan, then he must take heed to the Law of God. Remembering the Law of God is an essential step to entering our Canaan as well. Notice what the Lord said to Joshua about the Law and how this applies to our lives today.

> 1. v. 7—He was to keep the Law: He was to do everything the law said to do, not turning from it the least bit.

> 2. v. 8—He was to meditate on the Law: Day and night, his mind was to be occupied with the Law. He was to love it and let it fill his heart and mind. This was in order that his life might be centered in the Law and therefore in the will of God!

> 3. vv. 7, 8—He was to be successful and prosper by honoring the Law: God's promises to Joshua were that if he lived his life around the Law of God, God would prosper him and make him very successful.

There is a rhema word here for those on the Canaan odyssey. First, Christians today or in any century have never been under the Mosaic Law. Christians everywhere should rejoice that we are under the new covenant, which is a better covenant. The better covenant is the Gospel Covenant—the covenant of grace. That being so, some will think that because we are not under the Mosaic Covenant of Law, we are free to do whatever we want. Such is far from the truth. The Christian who is under the covenant of grace is still under law! For if there were no law, there would be no need for grace. In Gal. 6:2, we read: "Bear ye one another's burdens, and so fulfill the LAW OF CHRIST." (Emphasis mine) The venerable apostle Paul addresses this question in Romans 6. Having assured the Roman Christians that they were not under the law, he said in verse 1:

> "What shall we say then? Shall we continue in sin, that grace may abound? GOD FORBID. How shall we that are dead to sin live any longer therein."
>
> (Emphasis mine)

The word law here is the word "nomos" which refers to the gospel of Jesus Christ. While the text is an Old Testament text, the principle is a universal one. If we seek God, and that right early, He will bless us. The Joshua 1:8 principle is clearly seen in the Gospels. In Matt. 6:33, we read:

> "But seek ye FIRST the kingdom of God, and his righteousness; and ALL THESE THINGS shall be added unto you."

Clearly, the Law of Christ is demanding. In John 15:14, we read: "If you love me, keep my commandments." Now, we are not free to sin with impunity. We are most certainly under Law to Christ. Having said that, I hasten to add, Christians can walk in prosperity and victory if they would follow the principle God gave to His preacher Joshua. Develop a love for the word of God.

Let it dwell and rule in your hearts! If we do not, our spiritual life will be weak, sickly, and ineffective. However, if you choose to stay in the word, you are well on your way to reaching Canaan and entering into your spiritual victory.

The Call to Courage in Leadership—Paired with all God's instructions the Lord God had called Joshua to do, there was more. Three times God Himself encourages Joshua to be strong and courageous! These words carry the idea of "standing firm and strong in the face of opposition." Joshua, the preacher-prophet, would need great courage to face the enemies of Israel and lead the people to victory in the Promised Land. God's challenge to Joshua is for him to stand! That is the clarion call to all gospel preachers today. Not only must the leader of God's people stand, the preacher must also be set as in concrete for the defense of the gospel of Christ! There is a truism that is here: "He that will not stand for something will fall for anything!"

The rhema word suggested here for the twenty-first century preacher today is that he must internalize, through his faith in Christ Jesus, his need to stand for truth and veracity. He then needs to make sure that his people understand their great need to stand for the Lord. The preacher who is observant sees Christians all around him falling by the wayside.

As did Joshua, the twenty-first century preacher must also have a word from the Lord. He must take that word to the people because he is a provocateur. He must motivate them to be moved in the depths of their souls to stand firm for truth and veracity. He must move them to renew their commitment to the Lord and say, "By God's help, I'll stand and not fall all the days of my life!" We need women and men of God in churches today who will stand up and speak out against humanism, modernism, and secularism.

The preacher-provocateur needs to remember and recite constantly to the people Paul's admonition in I Cor. 15:58 and Eph. 6:10–17. If the church is going to be prepared to cross Jordan, the preacher man must take seriously his call to service.

THE PREACHER–PROPHET PROVOCATEUR CHALLENGES THE PEOPLE

The preacher-prophet provocateur has received his challenge from the Lord. Immediately and without hesitation, the preacher goes to the people. In the preceding section, I dealt with the difference between going to God on behalf of the people and going to the people on behalf of God. Joshua goes to the people with a word from the Lord. He tells them the time has arrived to take their land. There can be seen, in his challenge to the people, two dynamics in preparation to cross over Jordan:

- The Challenge to Readiness
- The Challenge to Responsibility

The Challenge to Readiness—Joshua tells the people the time had come to get ready to go into Canaan and claim the land. For forty years these Israelites had been looking forward to this day. Now that the day had arrived there were some things that they had to do. The Lord told them to prepare some foodstuff. In Joshua 1:10–11, we read:

> "¹⁰*Then Joshua commanded the officers of the people, saying,* ¹¹*"Pass through the host, and command the people,*

> *saying, Prepare you victuals; for within three days ye shall pass over this Jordan, to go in to possess the land, which the LORD your God giveth you to possess it."*

It is well to note here that for forty years they had been eating manna, but the diet was about to change. Manna was desert food and sufficient for desert wandering, but manna will not suffice for dwelling in Canaan! They were getting ready to cross over and go into a new land. That being so, the diet must change. Israel was about to move up and into something better. They were going to another level! They were going to a land flowing with milk and honey. What had sustained them in the desert was not going to be able to sustain them in the land of blessing!

The Christian today who has a mighty Jordan to cross in his or her life will do well to pay attention to this ancient story for some present-day learning. Before we can take on the mighty onrush of chilly Jordan, we must prepare. The way we live must change. The way we think must change. The things we feed on must change. The entire scope of our lives must be altered to adjust to life in Canaan.

Those who refuse to make that transitional shift (discussed elsewhere in this volume), will not cross Jordan successfully. This is why so many Christians never enjoy the abundant and victorious Christian life in Christ Jesus. They refuse to rid themselves of humanism, modernism, and secularism. They never make the transitional shift to living in spiritual victory.

Our success in whether we walk in victory or defeat depends directly on whether we walk by a new set of rules and Christian principles (see Rom. 6:4; Col. 3:1–10). Two crucial questions to ask as you read this are: "Is there anything in me I need to purge to get ready for Canaan?" and "Is there anything in me that the Devil can use?" Satan fights God through us. We must not allow the Devil to get an advantage on God by using us.

The Challenge to Responsibility—The preacher-prophet moves from challenging the people to get ready to being responsible. We observe Joshua addressing the tribes of Reuben, Gad, and the half tribe of Manasseh. These tribes had previously received permission from Moses to remain east of the Jordan, just outside of the Promised Land. The motivation for this request had to do with these tribes wanting grazing land for their cattle (Num. 32:1, 4, 16). Joshua stipulated this permission but he reminded them that they had promised to fight alongside their brethren until the land was conquered (Deut. 3:12–20). These tribes were challenged to remember their promise and to aid the nation until victory was secured. While they were permitted to settle in a land of prosperity, they were also in a land of danger!

History records years later that when the Assyrian army attacked from the east, these tribes were the first to go away into captivity. These two and one-half tribes did not learn the lesson played out years earlier in the life of Lot, who was the nephew of Abraham. From the biblical record, note the following text: "And when Lot looked and saw that the plains of Jordan was well watered, he pitched his tent TOWARD SODOM!"

In this ancient story we are afforded yet another rhema word. How many times have we seen this same scenario played out in the lives of many Christians? Christians who are more concerned about making a living than they are about making a life! Their primary motivation is getting ahead in life. They are more materially minded than they are spiritually minded. We could call them "borderline Christians." These are those who have obeyed the Lord Jesus Christ and have received deliverance, but have refused to go forward. They do not get involved in the ongoing ministry of the church. They give sparingly and sporadically. They come to worship infrequently and show up for fellowship and concerts. They play around the edges. They will cry aloud when they are attacked, but refuse to get involved when the church is at war with sin and Satan!

The call is to responsible Christianity. The call is to line up with the will of God for your life. If you expect to handle your Jordans and enter into Canaan, you cannot play around the edges of Canaan. To do so is to subject yourself to the possibility of soon falling out (Acts 20:9)! This must be the message of the preacher who has a word from the Lord.

The People's Response to the Preacher-Prophet Provocateur
- They Commit Themselves to a Life of Surrender
- They Commit Themselves to a Life of Submission
- They Commit Themselves to a Life of Separation

They Commit Themselves to a Life of Surrender—Joshua, the preacher-prophet, delivers the word of the Lord to the people. He does it without changing, perverting, or diluting it. He did it without fear or favor. When the people heard the word they responded! What did they do? They made their stand with the Lord. Not only did they make their stand with the Lord, they promised absolute obedience and surrender to the will of God. In Joshua 1:16, we read:

> "And they answered Joshua, saying, All that thou commandest us we will do, and whithersoever thou sendest us, we will go."

A wonderful rhema word emerges here. We see how spiritual victory is achieved. It is through total commitment to God. It is through total and absolute surrender of every level and area of our lives to the will of God and to His divine leadership. For us to do anything less will adversely hinder the move of God in our lives. Too often, we find ourselves imitating the actions and behavior of the men described in Luke 9:57–62. The will of God for our lives is that we surrender our will and follow Him to victory. In Ps. 37:5, we read:

> *"Commit thy way unto the LORD; trust also in him; and he shall bring it to pass."*

What the ancient text is saying to us today is very clear and simple. Commit and make a complete surrender to God, and rest assured He'll lead us through the chilly Jordans of our life.

They Commit Themselves to a Life of Submission—Inherent in the personal commitment of ancient Israel to God was also a commitment to the preacher-prophet. They not only promised to follow God and His divine leadership, Israel also promised to follow the leadership of God's man. Just as they had followed that great preacher-prophet Moses, they committed themselves to following Joshua.

From this second power point on the responding commitment of the people to the preacher-prophet emerges a biblical certainty. It is certain that the Bible teaches evangelistic authority. The office of the evangelist is just as much an office as the office of a bishop. The congregation should respect the evangelist and his office. Coupled with respect, the congregation is duly obligated to follow him as he follows God's will for the church.

There is, of course, a higher authority that every Christian must acknowledge. We must submit to the sovereignty and leadership of God. Congregational inertia can be traced to intrinsic rebellion in the hearts of Christians against authority. This rebellion is innate. None of us like to be told what to do. This attitude stems from Christians not knowing that they are in the service of God. The early Christians understood their theological status. In Romans 6:17–18, we read:

> *"17But God be thanked, that ye WERE THE SERVANTS of sin, but ye have obeyed from the heart that form of doctrine which was delivered you. 18Being then made free from sin, ye became the SERVANTS of righteousness."*

In II Cor. 12:11, we read: "I am become a fool in glorying." The venerable apostle Paul in his letter to the church at Phillipi said in Phil 2:5–7):

> *"5Let this mind be in you, which was also in Christ Jesus: 6Who, being in the form of God, thought it not robbery to be equal with God: 7But made himself of no reputation, and took upon him the form of a servant, and was made in the likeness of men."*

These passages, among many others, make clear how the Christian should see himself and herself in the service of God. What Paul is declaring in these passages is the idea of our being servants. Being a servant, our response to the word of the Master is, "Speak Lord, thou SERVANT hearest." When we were saved we "became" servants of God. As servants, we will more readily follow God and the human leadership of the church, as they follow Him.

Being a slave, a servant, we have no personal rights or privileges except those given us by God Himself. Our entire duty can be summed up in one word—submit. If you are ever going to cross Jordan and get to Canaan, you must submit and commit your ways unto the Lord. The question you must answer at this moment is: "Am I holding things back from the Lord because of my own personal aggrandizement?

Jordan will roll back and Canaan will open, but only to those who are subject to the will of God. These will be all that commit themselves to a life of submission to Him.

They Commit Themselves to a Life of Separation—Finally, in preparation to cross, ancient Israel's commitment is put to the ultimate human test: a commitment to separate themselves from those in their midst who refused to comply with the commandments of the Lord. Israel was so committed to God's word and their intent of separation was so strong that they made a vow. They vowed to put to death anyone who rebelled against the leadership of Joshua. Ancient Israel knew that allowing rebellion in its midst was a sure way to guarantee defeat. In Joshua 1:18, we read:

> *"Whosoever he be that doth rebel against thy commandment, and will not hearken unto thy words in all that thou commandest him, he shall be put to death: only be strong and of a good courage."* (Emphasis mine)

For every Jordan crosser and Canaan traveler, herein is a rhema word from the ancient page. If you wish to walk in victory, you must practice separation in your lives as well. We must learn to separate ourselves from anything that would hinder or prevent us from having victory in our lives.

The act of separation is not applied discriminately. Separation could mean from certain people, in the way we dress, the way we talk, things we watch and do, where we work, how we think, and in many other areas of our lives. If it hinders our entrance into our Canaan, then it must go! To not do it is to invite defeat and, unavoidably, imminent danger. Now ask yourself this question: "Am I involved or entangled with anything that is holding me back from properly serving God?" If the answer is positive, you need to get that settled today! In I Cor. 6:14–17, we read:

> *14Be ye not unequally yoked together with unbelievers: for what fellowship hath righteousness with unrighteousness? and what communion hath light with darkness? 15And what concord hath Christ with Belial? or what part hath he that believeth with an infidel? 16And what agreement hath the temple of God with idols? for ye are the temple of the living God; as God hath said, I will dwell in them, and walk in them; and I will be their God, and they shall be my people. 17Wherefore come out from among them, and be ye separate, saith the Lord, and touch not the unclean thing; and I will receive you, 18And will be a Father unto you, and ye shall be my sons and daughters, saith the Lord Almighty.*

Preparing for an Ocular Display of Divinity

As over a million people stand looking out over a river, more than one mile wide with its waters overflowing its bank, what must be their thoughts? In this scene there must be a longing, a longing that stretched over forty years of wilderness wandering. They had waited so long, their hope had been deferred for forty years. I am reminded of my college literature class where I had to recite Langston Hughes's ***"What Happens to a Dream Deferred?"***

Jordan River

> *What happens to a dream deferred?*
> *Does it dry up*
> *Like a raisin in the sun?*
> *Or fester like a sore—*
> *And then run?*
> *Does it stink like rotten meat?*
> *Or crust and sugar over—*
> *Like a syrupy sweet?*
> *Maybe it just sags*
> *like a heavy load.*
> *Or does it explode?*

Late they had come to the Jordan— forty years later! A generation had passed on. The story they told their young, dating back to the covenant of Abraham, is now within reach. What happened to their dream of Canaan or the land that flowed with milk and honey? Deferred, but not dried up! With what longing eyes must the ancient people of God look upon the river, which they were soon to cross. Could it really be true that on tomorrow the boundary line would separate them from their inheritance no more?

By the Jordan the Israelites were encamped, and the command of the text sounded in their ears: "Sanctify yourselves." This was to be the people's preparation of God's work among them. The people must prepare themselves to stand in the glory of God's presence. Such was the requirement at the appearance of the Almighty on Sinai and before the wondrous shower of quails, and so afterwards for the battle of Ai; otherwise the Lord would break forth upon them.

There are times when we must sanctify ourselves for the special manifestation of the Divine. Elsewhere in this volume, the author will discuss the three postulates that will guarantee your Jordan to roll back (see "Jordan River—Chilly, Deep, and Cold").

In preparing for an ocular display of divinity we must understand the human dimension. The human condition is clearly expressed in these words of Joshua: sanctify yourselves. Here we are clearly seen as partners with God. God wishes to show us His power! He wants to show us that our extremity is His opportunity. But for Him to do that, we must do our part by sanctifying ourselves. What makes personal sanctification so crucial to an ocular display of divinity is that God will not perform His matchless power in us, through us, with us, without us, without it. So He calls us to be fellow workers with Him.

To sanctify oneself is to put away all that is alien to the divine life. We must consecrate ourselves unreservedly to God, give ourselves to Him unhesitatingly. Yield ourselves to Him as willing instruments in His hands. When we do this, we are not serving ourselves, but serving Him. Paul writes in Romans 12:1–2 and we read:

> *"¹ beseech you therefore, brethren, by the mercies of God, that ye present your bodies a living sacrifice, holy, acceptable unto God, which is your reasonable service. ²And be not conformed to this world: but be ye transformed by the renewing of your mind, that ye may prove what is that good, and acceptable, and perfect, will of God."*

The lesson in this ancient story is clear. Let us be up and about the business of sanctifying ourselves like the children of Israel did on the verge of crossing their Jordan. To the degree that we do it, it will be to that degree that we will see the glory of God. Such would then be the fulfillment of the duality of the command Paul gave to the church at Philippi. In Phil. 2:12, 13, we read:

> "*¹²Work out your own salvation with fear and trembling. ¹³For it is God which worketh in you both to will and to do of his good pleasure.*" (Emphasis mine)

***The Parting of and a Passage Through a Perilous River*—** The parting of the waters of Jordan and Israel's safe passage through this perilous river will show God's amazing grace. It will also show His power in divine deliverance. He can deliver us from our wandering in the wilderness of sin and evil and translate us into the regions of His promises. Astute preparation for this crossing is a precursor to possession of the land of Canaan. Crossing Jordan will be a clear statement of His people as they contemplate not only the raging Jordan, but also their coming encounter with the Ites in Canaan.

Jordan was to be crossed at the time of its overflowing. It is said that during the time of the overflowing, the lower level of the valley was filled with deep, slimy ooze. The river itself was found to be fourteen feet above its normal level. This overflowing was caused by the melting of the snows of Hermon, which then rushed down, filled Lake Huleh and its marshes, as well as Gennesareth, and caused the swelling of the Jordan. It was here, at Jordan, that God would manifest His own glory and man's insufficiency. Because it will be at the "time of harvest," God's magnificent glory and power will be much more magnified.

In the New Testament, we can see clearly this modus operandi in God's scheme of things in the raising of Lazarus from the dead. His sisters thought the death of their brother could have been prevented if Jesus had only come when they "sent unto Him." But Jesus tarried where He was until Lazarus died. Upon arriving outside the city limits of Bethany, Martha met Him. She exclaimed, "this death of our brother need not have occurred had you been here." But Jesus had said, "This sickness is not unto death." In other words, "This is not what that is about" (scriptural paraphrase by the author). Jesus was clearly saying, you do not understand the will of my Father, and clearly, you do not know who I am. But, "If thou wouldest believe, thou shouldest see the GLORY OF GOD."

The greater the problem, the greater the opportunity for God to do greater works and receive greater glory. Jesus chose to wait until Lazarus died. He knew His father would receive more glory from Lazarus being raised from the dead than Lazarus being raised from his sickbed.

God will part the waters of Jordan and give His people passage at harvest time, because it was the time of the harvest when Jordan would be swollen out its banks. The time of our greatest troubles is the time that God performs His greatest manifestation of power! Israel needed to learn this lesson because of what lie ahead. They needed to be aware that their God would make for them a way through deep waters just as "the swelling of the Jordan" will abate at His presence. The overflow of ungodliness "gives ground at His word." When He speaks, sorrow and distress flee away. For those whose paths may at times be crooked, to them He will be a God that makes crooked paths straight.

The good news for every Christian soul that has embarked on the Canaan road is: know without uncertainty, their God is our God, and that He is a mighty good God! He knows the end from the beginning. He never starts anything that He has not already finished. He looks at time and sees all time at one time. When He swears, He swears by Himself, for there is no other greater than He.

Chapter 5

The Terrestrial vs. The Temporal

And Temporary Testimony of the Tenancy of God

"Brethren, I count not myself to have apprehended: but this one thing I do, forgetting those things which are behind, and reaching forth unto those things which are before."
Phil. 3:13

Chapter V

The sign of God's presence with Israel was temporary, but His presence is permanent! This postulate emerges from the fact that the pillar of cloud, which had previously led them, does not precede them at the Jordan. To its guidance they hitherto had marched, and under its shadow rested. The sign of God's presence had been a sweet assurance and a constant augury of success. Now it had disappeared altogether from the history of Israel. They would cross Jordan under the guidance of the ark, and of that alone. God's presence remains with them, but the sign of it is withdrawn. The template remained, but the temporary testimony of the signs was withdrawn.

Today, we have His presence. He is ever with us and we know it is true because the Bible declares it! While we do not have an ocular display of divinity in our lives today, we must not conclude that divinity is not in us and with us. At our conversion deliverance, divinity comes down to us, anoints us and dwells with us and in us! We have divinity, but not the sign of it. It is normal for even modern Christian to desire a sign, including those of us who have been saved by the precious blood of Jesus. We want some assurance of acceptance over and beyond what the words of the Gospel convey. We tend to want some "leading providence" in addition to our sense of duty before we are moved to step in the chilly waters of our personal Jordans.

This story demonstrates that our God does not come to us in signs, He comes to us in, by, and through faith. It demonstrates to the lowly Christian that his faith might be construed as folly. We discover, in order to achieve success even where success seems hopeless, we should follow the Divine. We can have the waters of our Jordans parted for safe passage, but it is only by the work of faith that such human impossibilities can become possible.

They Who Are Ark–Led Are Well Led

We saw when Israel no longer had the pillar of cloud and fire, they had the "Ark of God," and just as the cloud in the wilderness led them, the Ark led them as well. Their responsibility was to follow the Ark! To the degree that they followed the ark, it was going to be to that degree that they were going to find the help they needed, and what they needed it for.

This is not the place to do a complete definitive dissertation on the Ark, except to say the following. It was:

1. A wonderful piece of sacred symbolism
2. A representation of the "mercy seat of God"
3. The receptacle for the Ten Commandments written on two tablets of stones
4. A representation of "law and mercy." It proclaimed God, a God of law and mercy, of gracious promises and enabling precepts, delivering men by the grace He gave, dignifying them by the duty He exacted!

The process of crossing this Jordan changed for Israel, as in every Jordan. At this Jordan, we will see a clear change from a physical and ocular sign of fire and a cloud. We observe now the symbol of mercy and of duty. This suggests to every modern day Jordan crosser, if you march in lock step, following the lead of the words of the Messianic Master, you will be well led!

Joshua had the people understand that they had not been this way before. The future is always unknown and uncertain, but only God knows and sees the future. The Ark was not new to the ancient people of God. As a matter of fact, they were familiar with it. But a new significance was given to the divinity and spirituality of the Ark. The Ark at the Jordan was going to take the place of the symbolism of the cloud and the fire they followed in their wilderness wandering.

Their navigation of the Jordan presented a new challenge. They who had been with the moving of the cloud were now at the instruction of God, obligated to wait for the moving of the Ark and its designated carriers. God was about to do a new thing in His leadership and guidance. His modus operandi was about to change.

God in His essential being does not change. Throughout biblical history God remained constant in dealing with His people. When God gives His people His law, He expects obedience and rewards the doers of His law; however, those who disobey, He punishes. In this, God is constant. He does not change, but we see His law changes.

Today, the Messianic Master clearly represents the Ark of God in our lives. We are called to follow Him. In John 14:6, we read:

"I am THE WAY, THE TRUTH, and THE LIFE: no man cometh unto the Father, but by ME." (Emphasis mine)

If we dare to follow Jesus as the ancient people of God followed the Ark through chilly Jordan, our safe passage is assured. The challenge to every saint of God is to focus on Jesus and not our Jordans. Only Jesus can successfully lead us across our Jordans. He is the modern day Ark of the Covenant. He has promised us that He will be with us not only at the Jordan, but "all the way even to the end of the world." To this degree, it is those who are Ark-led that are well led!

When, by faith, we allow God to rule in our hearts and allow the word of Christ to dwell in our hearts, we will know that the way we are going is the right way. Our duty then becomes very clear: we have to "walk ye in it." It is not enough to believe in the realization of our higher destiny through the events of life. We must fully realize our part in the fulfillment of our passage over Jordan.

Ark–led Christians are "word-led" Christians who will rally, fight, and do battle with Satan when some conscientious soul gets too close to denominationalism. Ark-led and word-led Christians will love every sinner with a view of showing him God's gracious plan for saving man.

The Ark must be held high! We must not let it touch the water! We must, if we are going to effectively deal with the Canaanites, believe and defend the "Ark of the Covenant." We must allow the words of the covenant to rule and dwell in our hearts. We must allow the Ark of the Covenant to become the center of our lives, both public and private. To do this is to safely cross over Jordan, for they who are Ark-led are nothing short of being well led!

Not Timid or Terrified About Terra Firma

God speaks to Joshua and tells him to give a message to the priests. The message to the priest was to "stand still" in the Jordan. The text said when they had reached the midst of the Jordan, the priests were to "stand firm on dry ground in the midst of the Jordan." They were not to be terrified of terra firma. These powerful words from God to Joshua to the people leap off the old ancient page! "Stand still in Jordan," and the priests "stood firm on dry ground in the midst of the Jordan"!

Here is the refrain that calms the savage beast within us. When we, as did Israel, have a direct confrontation with the Jordans of our lives, and we are bereft of any and all ideas as to how to cross, even when our faith may have urged us to step in and we followed that urging, yet and still we are at risk and we know it.

The law of possibility is still operating in our universe. There is the possibility of being drowned. There is the possibility of being pulled along by the undertow or sinking in the marshy floor of the river. But the still small voice of the "God of the whole earth, and the Living God" resonates in our spirit: "stand still, and stand firm." God knew that the shallow portions of the river would not be as feared as the middle of the river. So He instructs them, when you reach the midst (middle), "stand still and stand firm."

There is a point that will demand steadfastness in our journey to Canaan, but it is not the same for everyone. When you reach it, you will know it and when you do, it's here you must stand still and let God do His work!

There must not be any staggered steps, faltering, or wavering. Once the passage was begun and the journey started, there must not be any turning back or losing heart. There must not be any signs of uncertainty. To show unbelief would have the water return and destroy them ultimately.

This text suggests, among other things, the gravity and greatness of the responsibility that is every gospel minister. The people look to their minister for guidance and encouragement. The preacher could fail or falter in the work of contending for the faith. He could become derelict in the promotion and the promulgation of the grand old gospel story. If his trumpet gives out an uncertain sound, or if he falls back from his appointed task, it places God's church in spiritual jeopardy.

How many great works have died, souls been lost, and churches split because some local preacher did not stand firm in the waters of Jordan? How many ministers have taken off their ministerial garments for secular garments, walked away from the one true church, or refused to preach what they clearly knew was the truth! All because they could not or would not "stand still and stand firm" on terra firma in the midst of Jordan!

There is no question that crossing Jordan represents a transition. It's a transforming, a metamorphosis, and a clear and ocular move that is dictated by an inward and spiritual force. Jordan crossing represents a passing—a passing from one level of Christianity to another. It is a spiritual maturation process. Paul the apostle was clear in this regard. In Phil. 3:13, we read:

> *"Brethren, I count not myself to have apprehended: but this one thing, forgetting those things which are behind, and reaching forth unto those things which are before."*

Again, Paul uses himself to encourage us. In I Cor. 13:11, we read:

> *"When I was a child, I spake as a child, I understood as a child, I thought as a child: but when I became a man, I put away childish things."*

When Israel crossed the Jordan, they would be cut off from their old lifestyle. Those who crossed to inhabit the new land would begin a new era and a new beginning with a new identification. They left in the distance pagan Egypt and the lifestyle of the wilderness. As their exodus demanded a new resolve, Jordan would also demand the same. When the Red Sea closed back up, their old enemies and old life style were buried in those waters. So it will be at the crossing of the Jordan.

It is clear that at our conversion we cross over from our old life to a new life to walk in victory and righteousness. Have you been changed since you crossed over? Is the transition in your life so dramatic that those who observe us will stand in awe? Is your crossing so visible and socially impacted that the world accuses us of truly being "born again"? There is a certain "aboveness" about saints who have crossed their Jordans so that people observing us will be moved to exclaim, "truly these people must have been with Jesus."

Chapter 6

The Theological and Transitional shift demanded from deep and chilly Jordan

"O LORD, I know that the way of man is not in himself: it is not in man that walketh to direct his steps."
Jeremiah 10:23

Chapter VI

The scriptures are replete that suggest a transitional shift. In Jeremiah 10:23, we read:

> "O LORD, I know that the way of man is not in himself: it is not in man that walketh to direct his steps."

In Psalm 121:1–8, David suggests a theological shift in time of the swelling of our mighty Jordans.

> "^{1}I will lift up mine eyes unto the hills, from whence cometh my help. ^{2}My help cometh from the Lord, which made the heaven and the earth."

Jeremiah, the great prophet of God, suggests that something other than what we have or are doing must be replaced in order to deal with the Jordans of our lives. In Jer. 12:5, we read:

> "If thou hast run with the footmen, and they have wearied thee, then how canst thou contend with horses? and if in the land of peace, wherein thou trustedst, they wearied thee, then how wilt thou do in the SWELLING OF JORDAN?" (Emphasis mine)

Below are some mental shifts that must be made by Canaan travelers. These transitional shifts must be made for spiritual awareness. The shifts that Christians make at deliverance are changes made in the heart.

Doubt and Fear to Favor and Faith

A transitional and transforming shift from doubt and fear to favor and faith is a shift from the sinners' mindset to the mindset of a child of God. Saints who are transformed do not overwhelmingly concern themselves with secularism, humanism, and modernism. They, at conversion, have gone through a spiritual metamorphosis. They are certain where their supply and help come from. They now trust in a God who is a God of covenant integrity and who will always keep His promises.

Doubt, fear, terror, and dread are the enemies of joy, peace, and happiness in the kingdom of God. Fear is an enemy that we will meet on the road to Canaan. There is a cornucopia of fears that are indicative of the human condition: fear of falling, fear of high places, fear of flying, fear of rejection, fear of not being able to please others. When fear and doubt take over our lives we become socially, theologically, and spiritually useless. We become as Jesus described, "fit for nothing but to be cast out and trodden under the feet of men."

Fear and doubt not only render us useless, they affect our spiritual conversation. In the state of fear, we render ourselves inadequate to speak the language of faith. Fear, dread, and terror go even further; they render the Christian immobile and paralyzed. But when we believe the promise of God we can cast our burdens on Him and He will send release and favor. Our God is an awesome God. He was a God of "just enough for the day—come back tomorrow for more" for Israel in the wilderness. But for every Christian traveler on the Canaan road wilderness today, He is a God of "more than enough!"

If we will cast out fear and allow faith to enter we will enjoy his favor. His favor will allow us to walk in victory and righteousness and not in weakness and fear. This faith is "bestowed." It is a virtue that has to do with our transitional theological capacity to accept the transforming power of the Gospel of Jesus Christ. Normally, we as Homo sapiens are initially endowed at birth with five basic senses. But those of us who have been "born again" are endowed with an extra sense called "faith." This spiritual sense keeps doubts and fear at bay. With this faith every Canaan road traveler can rest assured that if fear knocks, faith will answer and there will be no one there!

Faith was the greatest characteristic of the Master. The word was constantly upon his lips:

"According to thy faith be it unto you..."
"Thy faith hath made thee whole..."
"Thy faith hath saved thee..."

What Faith Does:

- Faith believes, but doubt fears
- Faith creates, but doubt destroys
- Faith opens the door to all things desirable in life, but doubt closes it
- Faith excites and arouses our creative forces. It cracks open the door of ability.
- Faith is the divine messenger sent to guide men and women blinded by doubt and trepidation

The individual who cannot see the great designer behind the design, who does not see infinite intelligence behind all creation, cannot possess the sublime faith that it takes to reach the ultimate Canaan of our lives. No one can rise higher than his or her faith. We must learn how to possess our possession called faith. When we internalize faith and not fear, we then have it with us every waking moment of our lives. This being so, we will then have the potential necessary to deal with the Ites on our way to Canaan.

Hope to Certainty

We have already established that Canaan can be any positive goal of life, as well as a theological goal. This transition, semantically put, conveys hope to certainty. I'm reminded of Jessie Jackson's famous "Hope" speech. "Keep Hope Alive" is the anthem he bellows from platforms all over the nation. If I were to do a dissertation on hope in a setting other than a religious one, I would be scholastic. I would say that hope is what urges, agitates, and causes us to persevere. I would say that a better life, a better world, a better tomorrow depend on a better hope today. However, in deference to the subject at hand, I want to postulate that hope moves us to certainty. I am not saying hope turns into belief. The New Testament inverts these terms. In I Cor. 13, Paul writes, and we read:

> "And now abideth FAITH, HOPE, CHARITY, these three; but the greatest of these is CHARITY." (Emphasis mine)

In the economy of God, faith precedes hope. Faith is placed first because faith actualizes everything else. Faith makes real what we cannot see. According to scripture, hope holds. Hope is the anchor that holds because of what we see through our faith.

Many readers of these pages have been working on jobs and in employment for twenty years or more. What has held you to that job? What has gotten you out of bed for more than twenty years, rain, sleet or snow notwithstanding? You were anchored because of what your faith visualized and made real for you—your paycheck! As long as you could visualize the paycheck coming in, staying power was not a problem. If hope believes, it is because faith makes it real!

Many Christians are derelict in their Christian duties to God and the church. They blame this dereliction of duty on weakness when, in point of fact, it is not weakness that is the cause. The cause is a clear case of a non-visualizing faith! In the absence of an object, hope has nothing to which it can anchor. Jesus Christ is the Christian's object. If we, as Christians, would clearly visualize the cross and what happened there for us, we would then get anchored in Jesus. Once Jesus Christ becomes the object of our faith, Christian mobility is no longer a problem. We would give of our means, assemble and work in the ministry, unhampered and unhindered.

It is clear that Israel, at Jordan, believed God and, as the next chapter will show, followed His presence in the Ark through the midst of Jordan. Because of their faith, their hope was realized! The hymnologist Edward Mote was correct when he penned the hymn, *"The Solid Rock"* in 1834:

> *"My hope is built on nothing less*
> *Than Jesus' blood and righteousness*
> *I dare not trust the sweetest frame*
> *But wholly lean on Jesus' name.*
> *On Christ the solid rock I stand*
> *All other ground is sinking sand."*

GRUDGES AND ACCUSATIONS TO FORGIVING AND RECONCILIATION

Forgiveness is truly a Christian possession. As a matter of fact, it could well be considered one of the most important virtues of mature Christian development. There is an innate tendency to place blame on others when things do not go our way. We will not have a successful entrance into the land that flows with milk and honey unless we find release for our latent, negative feelings. Jealousy, envy and personal assessment of others enslave us. In the economy of God, personal judgment of others is not God-approved. Judgment, of course, is not exempted from the Christian construct. It is clear that Jesus in the gospels spoke on this subject. In Matt. 7:1–2, we read:

> *"1Judge not, that ye be not judged. 2For with what judgment ye judge, ye shall be judged: and with what measure ye mete, it shall be measured to you again."*

If one read only this verse, one could conclude, as some religionist do, that Christians should make no judgments. But that's not all that is said about Christian making judgment on others. In John 7:24, we read:

> *"Judge not according to the APPEARANCE, but judge RIGHTEOUS judgment."* (Emphasis mine)

The right to judge is given and the way we should not judge is forbidden. As long as the inspired word is our rule, we are commissioned to be the determiners of what is "truth" and what is "error." Jealousy, envy, and personal assessments must give way to forgiving and reconciliation. The old adage is still true: "to err is human, to forgive is divine." St. Frances Assisi was correct when he said:

"O brother man fold to thy heart thy brother.
Where pity dwells the peace of God is there.
To worship rightly is to love each other.
Each smile at him, each kindly deed, a prayer."

The source for the existence of jealousy and envy is clearly found in our mischaracterization of others. The reason for this is a lack of selfhood and self-love. Once you stop accusing and being jealous of others, you actually starve the life of negative emotions. We must make the transition no matter how difficult. To cross Jordan, we must free ourselves of all negativity. Failure to free yourself of negative emotions gives someone else the ascendancy in your life and the privilege of controlling you. If the Jordans of life are going to ever get crossed, we must let go and let God. Forgiveness is a possession that we must possess!

PHYSICALITY TO SPIRITUALITY

To successfully cross the Jordans that run chilly, deep, and cold in your life, serious spirituality is demanded. Scripture is clear on this question. David, the great psalmist of Israel said in Ps. 1:2:

"But his delight is in the law of the LORD; and in his law doth he MEDITATE day and night." (Emphasis mine)

Continuing, David says in Ps. 19:14:

"Let the words of my mouth, and the MEDITATION of my heart, be acceptable in thy sight, O LORD, my strength, and my redeemer." (Emphasis mine)

Paul, in his instructions to the young man, Timothy, exhorts him to the absolute need of meditation in the inspired word. In I Tim. 4:15, we read:

> *"MEDITATE upon these things; give thyself WHOLLY to them; that thy profiting may appear to all."*
> (Emphasis mine)

The word that is under discussion, "meditate," is the English translation of the Greek word "meletas." Its primary meaning is: (i) to care for; (ii) to attend to, practice. There is only one main reason for practice: to get better, to improve, or to be the best we can be. It is a mental, physical, and spiritual approach to the inspired word and things that are spiritual. It is getting us in the position to be overwhelmed by the divine word. It is crucial that Jordan crossers understand this principle. Emerging from this inspired principle is a tacit negation of physicality, and a serious pursuit of spirituality.

Many religious adherents today have more religion in their hands and feet than they have in their heads! Christianity is a "head" religion. Jesus said, "Ye shall KNOW the truth and the truth shall make you free." The emphasis is on knowledge in our heads rather than a shaking of the body. Christianity is not what you feel; it is a question of what you know.

John 8:32;	*"Ye shall know the truth..."*
Acts 20:29;	*"I know this..."*
Rom. 7:1;	*"I speak to them that know..."*
Rom. 7:18;	*"For I know that in me..."*
Rom 7:28;	*"We know that all things work..."*
II Cor. 5:1;	*"We know that if our earthly house..."*
Phil. 3:10;	*"That I may know Him..."*
I Tim. 3:15;	*"Thou oughtest to know how to behave..."*

I Jno. 2:3;	*"Hereby we do know…"*
I Jno. 3:14;	*"We know we have passed from death to life"*
I Jno. 3:24;	*"Hereby we know we know Him…"*
I Jno. 5:10;	*"We know that we are of God…"*
I Jno. 5:20;	*"That we may know Him…"*

Christians, because of what we know, do not show up to show out. Scripture indicates that the early Christians showed up for the show down! Purely physical activity will not get us across Jordan; rather, it's allowing the word to dwell in our hearts. It's about allowing God to rule in our hearts. Meditation is a vital possession that we must possess if crossing Jordan is going to be successful.

WHAT ARE YOU LABORING FOR *to* WHAT ARE YOU LIVING FOR

It is important that saints of God should always remember, as they make their way to Canaan, this one thing: there is a difference between your employment and your work! IBM may employ you, but you work for God! There is certainly nothing new about this principle, except that not many saints of God understand it. Since my high school days, I've heard this statement made in some form or another. For the purpose of this volume, I want to place it into the context of becoming a strong Canaan road traveler, and, at the same time, make it fundamental to this thesis. The same principle, unchanged, can be used to show the Christian's transitional process fundamental to achieving Canaan.

To cross Jordan, the spirit is going to have to take the ascendancy in us. Jesus Christ was very blunt and direct on this issue. In John 6:63, we read:

> "It is the spirit that quickeneth; the flesh profiteth NOTHING." (Emphasis mine)

Fleshly pursuits, supremely, is vain deceit. The flesh looks out for flesh. Flesh is only concerned with its gratification. The venerable apostle Paul wrote much about the place of the flesh in the Christian's scheme of things. In Rom. 8:1ff

> "¹There is therefore now no condemnation to them which are in Christ Jesus, who walk not after the FLESH, but after the SPIRIT. ⁵For they that are after the FLESH do mind the things of the FLESH; but they that are after the SPIRIT the things of the SPIRIT. ⁸...they that are in the flesh CANNOT PLEASE GOD. ¹²Therefore, brethren, we are debtors, not to the FLESH, to live after the FLESH. ¹³For if ye LIVE after the FLESH, ye shall die: but if ye through the SPIRIT do mortify the deeds of the body, ye shall LIVE. (Emphasis mine)

Clearly, we can see the "transitional concept" implicit in the above verses. Everyone is desirous of making a living, surviving, and providing for ourselves the essentials of life. But we cannot live our lives (all our lives) after the flesh, pursuing that which satisfies the flesh exclusively, for such is vanity and vexation of the spirit.

Israel could have refused to obey Joshua's command to go forward over Jordan. They could have taken the word of the ten spies. But they decided to accept transitional theology rather than traditional. As we will see, it would be transitional theology that caused them to line up, every man to his own tribe. The priests would take their place up front, leading with the Ark of the Covenant. It was transitional theology that caused Israel not to violate the holy space between them and the Ark of Covenant, and the priest carrying it. It was transitional theology that caused the priest to step in the waters of Jordan and, in the midst of the Jordan, to stand still! If we as Christians are to make a difference on the road to Canaan, we must resolve to become what Paul admonished us to become: transformed non-conformists (Rom. 12:1–2).

Making a living becomes secondary to every Christian Jordan crosser when making a life is an option. If we will, by faith, let God have the ascendancy in our lives and strive for the best that is in us, God will come. He will come and juncture with us at our point of need. He seeks such to worship Him. He seeks the man He can work through, because that's the man He sends His blessing to!

We must possess what the Lord has given and will give to every true believer that confesses Jesus Christ as Lord. The ability to make the transition from the secular to the sacred should be our daily practice. When our physical and mental abilities are needed we can use them for all our secular pursuits, but when the physical and mental cannot handle the breakers of the Jordan, we then make the transition to the level of the spiritual realm. And it is on this transitional level that we will meet God!

Confusion and Doubting to Certainty and Trust

What do you do when you do not know what to do? Israel had a problem, but God had a plan! Have you ever been at a place where you did not know what to do? Have you ever looked around you and no one looking at you could help you? Have you ever suffered from powerful migraine headaches because of pure anxiety? Have you ever had an anxiety attack, simply because you did not know what to do? Did that cause you to doubt? If for only a moment, did you doubt that you were going to make it?

The Journey to Canaan

Doubt your Christianity? Yea, even doubt God? This will be the case at the Jordan.

This has happened to me when I lost my son, whose death I have never gotten over. Those who have walked this road know whereof I speak. There is no question about my knowing and understanding the scriptural teaching on life and death. When one experiences the death of a beloved child, things seem to pale; one can't resist these questions that seem to loom in one's mind.

When Antonio passed, I found myself in a locked room with an open door. For those who have been there, you know the feeling of sitting in a locked room with an open door. These emotions, universal to all those who have been there, need no explanation; we relate in silence.

When I meet or talk to those who tell me that they have lost a child through death, I simply say, "I've been there." Immediately, there is a kinship. Common tears begin to flow because we've experienced being locked in a room with an open door. We have been locked in our emotions because of our lost one. The world, to us, stood still. Very little made sense. We were mummified with grief. We had become temporarily unable to deal with life. Doubt, uncertainty, and even anger filled our hearts.

Yet we knew what God had said in His word. Yet we clearly knew that the God that gives is the same God that takes. Yet we knew clearly that God never makes a mistake; He never makes an error! This knowledge is the open door. But grief has us locked in, and we find it unusually difficult to go through the open door. It is not that we do not believe God, or that we do not see the open door, but grief has so locked us in the room that we cannot seem to get up and pass through the open door. So we give in to the "lostness," which is a normal human reaction. If during these times we are not careful, lingering doubt will separate and sever our relationship with God.

Jesus showed momentary and temporary grief at the grave of Lazarus. This is not to say that the Master was in doubt, rather, He was showing normal human grief. These human tendencies and other mundane things cause us to doubt. But the question is, what do we do when we do not know what to do? I suggest seven things:

1. Trust in the Lord
2. Lean not unto thine own understanding
3. In all thy ways acknowledge Him
4. Honor the Lord with thy substance
5. Be not afraid
6. Devise not evil against thy neighbor
7. Strive not with a man without cause

These principles are taken from Proverbs 3:5–6; 9–10; 25–30. If our Jordans are to be crossed, we must replace doubt with trust. Trust, absolute trust in God is a Christian possession, and we must learn to possess it. Like Job, we must trust in God, in spite of how things look. This is the key to peace and plenty.

Chapter 7

JordanN RiveR

chilly, deep and cold

"If thou hast run with the footmen, and they have wearied thee, then how canst thou contend with horses? and if in the land of peace, wherein thou trustedst, they wearied thee, then how wilt thou do in the SWELLING OF JORDAN?"

Chapter VII

Because of their unbelief, Israel was sentenced to wander in the wilderness for forty years. The years had now expired and the children of Israel were poised to enter into Canaan land. They were ready to claim their inheritance in the land of promise, but before they can enter Canaan, they must first get past one final, major obstacle—the Jordan River! Once they crossed the Jordan they would enter into the central campaign for absolute possession.

Normally, this crossing would not have presented much of a problem, since the Jordan was only 100 feet wide at Gilgal where they crossed. Those who have been there during the harvest time tell us that the Jordan swells to an impossible width of more than one mile! It was more than fifty times wider than it normally would have been when Israel arrived. There was no way they could cross this river on their own! However, it seems that God always does things in such a way that no man can boast of having done them on his own. They needed supernatural help and this crossing would be no exception. You see, God brought them to the Jordan River at the time of harvest (4:15); to prove their efforts would be useless. When they crossed at the time of harvest, He was saying to them that, while they may want to believe they could cross themselves, the evidence points to another source of help: it was supernatural help!

There are principles emerging here in this story that demand recognition. The same principles used to get God's ancient people across Jordan in that distant yesterday more than 3,000 years ago will work for every Jordan crosser today. Needing a word of faith to cross over, there are two postulates that were involved in the crossing of mighty Jordan. Two postulates, if considered properly, are guaranteed to unblock your mind and your way, and eventually cause your Jordan to roll back! First:

It Involved a Challenge

The Jordan crossing of ancient Israel involved challenge. When it came time for the people to move forward to cross Jordan, God had a message that they needed to hear. From the words they heard, they were challenged to do two very important things, which were designed to help them follow the Lord better. These are the very same things every Jordan crosser need to hear today that will help us to follow the Lord better as we cross our mighty Jordans. First, they were challenged to:

1. Watch God

Note carefully that the Ark of the Covenant is mentioned seven times in Chapter Three. The Ark, as you will note, was constructed to symbolize the presence and power of God. The Ark was a replica of the tabernacle and its three compartments. The holy of holiness was the dwelling place of God and His glory rested there. The Ark represented God's presence in their midst. It was tantamount to His move. When the Ark moved, God moved. When God moved, they were to move. When the Ark stopped, God stopped. When God stopped, they were to stop. No one was allowed to precede, come near, or touch the Ark, except for members of the tribe of Levi.

Therein lies a valuable reason for those of us who will dare to travel the road to Canaan. We will do well when we face our Jordans on our way to Canaan, to face squarely our crisis. When we are in need of direction in our lives, we must be sensitive to the movement of the Lord in our lives and around us. In Eph. 5:15, we read:

> *"See then that ye walk circumspectly, not as fool, but as wise, redeeming the time, because the days are evil."*

The second subsection of postulate one is as crucially important as the first. They were challenged to:

2. *Follow God*

When ancient Israel saw the Ark of the Covenant move, they knew they were to move, "leave your place, and go after it." Not only were they to watch God, they were to move when He did. They were to pursue God! There is a Rhema word here for all Jordan crossers. The rhema word is simply this—there will come a time in our sojourn when just knowing what God says, or what God is doing, is not enough. There will come a time when we must leave our place and go after Him. The demand may dictate that we leave our comfort zone, our relatives and friends, and go after the Lord. Paul spoke to this issue. In Col. 2:8, we read:

> *"Beware lest any man spoil you through philosophy and vain deceit, AFTER the tradition of men, AFTER the rudiments of the world, and not AFTER Christ."*
> (Emphasis mine)

Israel was about to follow the Ark through a river called Jordan, running chilly, deep, and cold, and more than one mile wide! Surely this was not an easy task, but it certainly was a necessary one if they were to ever reach Canaan, the land of promise.

I suggest that following God is not always easy, as we shall see in subsequent chapters. However, we shall also see that it will certainly be the best thing to do. If we will ever get to our Canaan, we must resolve to follow God when He is leading and obey His instructions when He is guiding.

3. Honor God

Not only must Israel watch and follow God, they must also honor God. We note in this postulate that the ancient people of God are instructed to stay at least 3,000 feet behind the Ark. This distance had a rhema purpose. While we may not know what the divine and definitive purpose of this command is, here is what we do know. At this distance, we can easily see what is happening ahead of us. We also know that God wanted and had decreed that only the Levites were permitted near the Ark.

Also emerging from the text is the idea that the Lord does not want to be our buddy! This distance places us in a position far enough away yet close enough to demand holy reverence and holy fear of the Lord in our hearts. We must never permit a spirit of familiarity to cheapen our walk with the Lord. Regardless of how we may be blessed by God's grace, we are still sinners saved by His amazing grace. Watch God, follow God, and honor God. Let Him lead you, let Him guide you, and pray much that you may know the difference!

It Involved a Command

Jordan would be crossed! Ancient Israel would march untouched by the enemy across the mighty Jordan. But they would not cross absent clear commands from the God of Abraham, Isaac, and Jacob. The commands must be obeyed or Jordan will not roll back. The voice of the God of the universe reverberates from glory. He commands the preacher-prophet provocateur the following:

Jordan River—Chilly, Deep, and Cold

1. *"Arise, go over this Jordan"* (1:2)
2. *"Be strong and of good courage"* (1:6)
3. *"Meditate in this book of the Law day and night"* (1:8)
4. *"Be not afraid, neither be thou dismayed"* (1:9)
5. *"When the priests shall come to the brink of the water of Jordan, stand still in Jordan"* (3:8)

These commands came directly from God to Joshua. If Jordan is going to be crossed the preacher-prophet provocateur must do his part. He must not tinker or tamper with the testimony. The preacher will be tested based on his willingness to convey to the people the divine testimony. Joshua now goes to the people and gives them the commands necessary to get them across Jordan.

1. *"Prepare ye food for the crossing"* (1:11)
2. *"Whosoever rebel against any command will be put to death!"* (1:18)
3. *"When you see the Ark of the Covenant move, then ye shall remove and go after it"* (3:3)
4. *"Leave a space of half-mile between you and the ark* (3:4)
5. *"Sanctify yourselves"* (3:5)
6. To the priests Joshua said, *"take up Ark of the Covenant and pass over before the people"* (3:6)
7. *"Come hither, and hear the words of the Lord your God"* (3:9)

These commands from God to the preacher-prophet provocateur, and from the preacher-prophet provocateur to the people posit a crucial lesson. First, they become the conditions that had to be met for Israel to successfully cross the mighty Jordan. The question of congregational inertia is herein answered. Not only have we found an answer for congregational inertia, but also is a prevention measure for the onset of congregational conflict.

Ancient Israel in its preparations to cross over Jordan was told to look up, clean up, and line up! Look up to God—worship, honor, and respect. Clean up— sanctify yourselves, and line up— every one get in their particular place, every man to his own tribe. The lack of Christians in their place is one of the cardinal reasons for church conflict and congregational inertia. Too many Christians out of ministry, committee, evangelism, assembly, church school, and worship gives rise to idle time, personal encroachment, and bickering. The same is true for congregations that ignore the command to look up, clean up, and line up. Any refusal to obey the commands and instructions from God will render us unable to handle the flooded waters of an overflowing Jordan. In I John 3:22, we read:

> *"And whatsoever we ask, we received of Him, because we KEEP HIS COMMANDMENTS, and do those things that are pleasing in His sight."* (Emphasis mine)

Crossing Jordan demanded and involved the keeping of commands. Lest the reader assumes that a simple legal adherence to the law of God is sufficient, I offer my views. Careful note should be given to the fact that the Lord did not stop the flow of the Jordan until the priests' feet were actually in the water. They were called upon to exercise their faith first. No social, domestic, financial, or spiritual Jordan will be crossed for any child of God in the absence of faith (Heb. 11:1, 6).

Israel obeyed the commands of God and chilly Jordan had to roll back and stand up in a heap! God had said to Israel, "CROSS THIS JORDAN! You and all this people, to the land which I am giving to them, to the sons of Israel" (1:2). He was further assured, "Every place on which the sole of your foot treads, I have given it to you, just as I spoke to Moses" (1:3).

Jordan River—Chilly, Deep, and Cold

Next comes the vanquishing of the last obstacle that stood between ancient Israel and Canaan: the mighty Jordan, running chilly, deep, and cold. When you read the next chapter, you will experience the physical, emotional, and spiritual ecstasy of the breaking of the waters of a mighty river called Jordan!

It Involves a Commitment

We are poised here at the banks of the Jordan! Looking back through the corridors of time on the black hordes of our minds, the scene is awesome. Skeptics would scoff at such a scene and call the anticipation of ancient Israel ridiculous! It is here at the Jordan that the preacher-prophet provocateur stands at the brink of this mighty river with its water lapping the shore and calls out to the waiting people of God.

We can hear the clarion call as it resonates and reverberates through that silent and still audience of over one million people. In Joshua 3:9–13, we read:

> *"⁹...COME HITHER, and HEAR THE WORDS of the LORD your God. ¹⁰And Joshua said, Hereby ye shall know that the living God is among you, and that he will without fail drive out from before you the CANAANITES, and the HITTITES, and the HIVITES, and the PERIZZITES, and the GIRGASHITES, and the AMORITES, and the JEBUSITES. ¹¹Behold, the ARK of the covenant of the Lord of all the earth PASSETH OVER before you INTO JORDAN. ¹²Now therefore take you twelve men out of the tribes of Israel, out of every tribe a man. ¹³And IT SHALL COME TO PASS, as soon as the soles of the feet of the priests that bear the ark of the LORD, THE LORD OF ALL THE EARTH, shall rest in*

the waters of Jordan, that the WATERS OF JORDAN shall be CUT OFF from the WATERS that come down from above; and they shall stand upon an heap."

(Emphasis mine)

Let the word go forth from these pages to every nook and cranny in every place, that when the Lord prognosticates a future or present course of action, it shall come to pass. Therefore let the word of our God rule in the heart of His people everywhere. Let every gospel preacher take heart; God will part your Jordans. God promised that on this day Jordan would roll. On that promise Israel could put their name and claim it as already done. In Joshua 1:6–9, God assures the preacher that the trip across the Jordan will be successful. In v.9 we read:

"Have not I commanded thee [preacher]? BE STRONG and of a good courage; be not AFRAID, neither be thou dismayed: for the LORD thy God is with thee whithersoever thou goest." (Emphasis mine)

They must not tremble but trust God at His word. Israel had to meet God on that level in order to handle that mighty river. It was on that level and that level only they had to commit to Him. If they committed to Him on that level they would unhesitatingly follow Him into the unknown adventures of that river.

The reader should feel the intensity of mind and spirit as the preacher methodically, without fear or favor, outlined the strategy for the crossing. He explained the place and the position of the Ark of the Covenant. As has already explained in previous chapters, the place and position of the Ark was crucial. The Ark of the Covenant symbolized God's presence with His people. Its position was to be in front of the people. This full-frontal position indicated God is leading. That being so, the Lord would not only lead, He would be the first to cross the Jordan. The people's responsibility was to follow Him. They must not get in front of God or His chosen leadership. In everything, let God lead, rule, and dwell in our hearts by faith.

When the feet of priests, carrying the Ark of the Covenant, touched the water, it's at that moment, instantaneously, that mighty river—overflowed as it was—began to dry up! And that is exactly what happened! What a scene! What a picture of supernatural power! The priest came to the edge of the water and stood still in the river. That mighty river did not only dry up where they were standing. Sixteen miles upstream at Adam, it began to pile up in a heap! The waters were completely cut off and the people crossed over the river. What a magnificent sight! The priests of God, standing in the midst of the Jordan, holding high the Ark of the Covenant, standing firm on dry ground, till all of Israel had crossed over into Canaan land!

Our Rhema Word

What a feeling! What a powerful thought! To know that the same God that led ancient Israel across that great river leads us across our Jordans. This was a new experience for Israel, an experience that came more than forty years after its initial pursuit.

How many times do we face new experiences in our lives? Jordans that seem to swell and overflow in our lives. Experiences we waited patiently for God to take control of one way or the other. Then we realized that we had not committed ourselves to Him on His level. We had not, like the priests, stepped by faith into the water. We had not totally released ourselves unto God. If your Jordan has not rolled back and nothing has changed in your walk with God, it may be that God is waiting for you to get your feet wet. Step in the water by complete faith in Him.

The second rhema word speaks to a passage, our passage from one level of Christian faith to another (Rom. 1:17). This concept was dealt with in the section on "Theological and Transitional Shifts." When you cross your Jordan, your life takes on a new dimension with a new mindset and identification. In crossing Jordan, Israel had committed their lives to God. When the last person in that great aggregation of people placed his or her foot on the new shore and Jordan River returned to its normal flow, something new happened. They were completely cut off from wilderness wandering, their old life and lifestyles. They were now, and for all practical purposes, a new people walking in a new direction with new orders to do new things.

The third rhema word to all Jordan crossers today: "keep your eyes on Jesus." Jesus has gone before us and prepared the way. We need only to follow Him. If we follow Him, He will make the floor of our Jordan and its waters to dry up. If we follow Him as Israel followed the Ark, He will lead us into a deeper understanding of life.

Do you face a chilly, deep, cold, and slimy Jordan today? This story opens a door of opportunity for you. Whatever the burden you are carrying, if you as a Christian or sinner would commit to Jesus—our Ark of the Covenant—He will deliver you (I Tim. 1:15). Commit to Him, follow Him, and you will, without doubt, enter into that spiritual Promised Land. Even here, as we will see in the next chapter, God is at work. He did not forsake Israel, and he will not forsake us today. Make that decision today to step in the water, by faith, and watch God work in your life.

CHAPTER 8

The Anatomy of the Jordan River Crossing

"Have you lost your desire since you found out what it requires?"

Chapter VIII

What do you see as a universal literary motif as you read this ancient story of The Jordan on the ancient page? Clearly, three postulates emerge. Having seen other postulates presented in the preceding section, look now at a universal literary motif. In verse 15, Joshua informs the people of God that God would give them this good land beyond Jordan. He informs them they would return unto this good land to "possess it and enjoy it." That's good, but a slight problem faced them—the Jordan River. So the first universal postulate suggests that::

There Was a Problem

This was literally a big problem. They were facing a real river! This river was more than one mile wide, and in addition to that, at least two million people had to cross over. Add to that the fact they could neither build a bridge (there was not enough time or material), nor were there were any boats to transport two million people. Militarily, they would have been sitting ducks for their enemies. Yes, there was a problem, and the only way around it was through it! But let's be clear, man's extremities are God's opportunities. Israel saw a real human problem, but God saw an opportunity.

So many times we are faced with what we think are insurmountable problems. To us, they look large and impossible to overcome. To us, our problems drive us to irrational conclusions. Sometimes they cause us to conclude there is no way around, through, over, or past our problems. How many times have we reacted like the ten spies that were sent to spy out the land?

Returning—with the exception of Joshua and Caleb—they said, "we have sized up our problem and we think it is more than we can do" (Num. 13:31–33). Their problem is our problem when we face what we think is an impossible Jordan: we forget God! When we see problems, God sees solutions!

God does not see things like Israel saw things. Israel saw the expanse of a Red Sea—God saw a throughway. Israel saw a rock—God saw a fountain. Israel looked up and saw a blue sky—God saw a kitchen and rained down bread from heaven. God does not see things the way we see things. When we look at things and say, "There is no way," God looks at the same thing and says, "Follow me; I have a plan!"

Our responsibility in crossing our difficult Jordans is being able to differentiate between when God is leading and when God is guiding. When God is leading, He's in front and we are following! When God is guiding, He is behind us (got our back) and we are in front. It is more difficult for us as human Christians when God is guiding. When God is guiding, we are in front! To the degree we know the difference, it will be to the degree that we can go through our Jordans. Yes, Israel saw a problem, but God is saying to Israel and His people of all times, "Follow me; I have a plan!"

There Was a Plan

God always has a plan for all your Jordans. To ancient Israel, He said, "When the feet of the priests enter Jordan, I am going to part the waters and lead you through on dry ground!" In Joshua 3:13, we read:

> *"And it shall come to pass, as soon as the soles of the feet of the priests that bear the ark of the LORD, the Lord of all the earth, shall rest in the waters of Jordan, [that] the waters of Jordan shall be cut off [from] the waters that come down from above; and they shall stand upon an heap."*

This is the plan; it was God's plan. It did not matter that Jordan had swollen. It did not matter that the river had risen to more than fourteen feet above its original level. It did not matter that it had "overflowed all its banks." This swelling of the Jordan was caused by the melting of the snows of Hermon, which then rushed down and filled all the tributaries, Galilee, and the marshes. This resulted in the swelling of the Jordan.

Israel had to move deliberately, under the direction of Joshua, down to the brink of the river. They had to wait in calm expectation for the salvation of the Lord. Here again, we get another chance to watch God work! In the passage of the Red Sea, an intermediate agent was employed to bring about the results. "The Lord caused the sea to go back by a strong east wind" (Ex. 14:21). There would be no indication of anything of that kind here. It would be a direct exercise of the wonder-working hand of God. In the Red Sea case, a natural agent is used supernaturally because nothing can and will intervene between the supernatural cause and the visible effect.

We see something very important emerging here, other than the wonder-working hand of God; it's in this plan that an everlasting principle evolves. What I see is the fact that the waters are not going to part until the priests, who will be carrying the Ark, step into the water. In a word, it will take a step of faith by the obedient people of God following Him for the waters of Jordan to part.

A rhema word cries out for recognition. Too often, we want the Lord to just fix everything in our lives for us. We do not want to have to make any moves or decisions. Our faith in Him lies dormant. That is not how God ferries us across and through our Jordans. The Hebrew writer said, "Without faith, it is impossible to please God" (Heb. 11:6). God requires us to take a step of faith in order that we might see our Jordan parted. God has a plan, but for His plan to work, it requires faith on the part of His people! The same is true for you and me. As long as we are trying to solve our own problems we are not walking by faith. It is only when we turn loose of the reins of the problems, step away from them, and let the Lord have them that we will see it taken care of, for His glory and His honor. It must not ever be about what we can do, but always what the Lord is able to do through us (Eph. 3:20).

There Must Be a Performance (vv. 16–17)

Not only was there a problem and a plan, but emerging from the text is a demand for a performance. When the priests entered into that raging, chilly, deep, and cold Jordan River, it parted and God opened a path of dry ground through the waters for His people. In 3:16, we read:

> "¹⁶*The waters which came down from above stood [and] rose up upon an heap very far from the city Adam, that [is] beside Zaretan: and those that came down toward the sea of the plain, [even] the salt sea, failed, [and] were cut off: and the people passed over right against Jericho. ¹⁷And the priests that bare the ark of the covenant of the LORD stood firm on dry ground in the midst of Jordan,*

and all the Israelites passed over on dry ground, until all the people were passed clean over Jordan."

Let us not miss this! After forty years of wilderness wandering, the first step was about to be taken and Israel was getting ready to cross the Jordan! Before we deal with the actual crossing, as a precursor we are afforded a glimpse. Verse 16 says the waters backed up to the city of Adam. This was some twenty miles north of where the children of Israel were crossing. God was going to make them a path through the water that would be more than adequate for His people to get through.

What a mighty God our God is! We must never forget that faith honors God and God honors faith! The rhema word is clear. The God who did this great thing for Israel is still the same God we serve today. What He did then, He is still able to do today. Regardless of the circumstances, He is still God and He still can.

If we will pause for a moment and look back over our own lives, the scriptural minutes are clear. How many times has the Lord opened your Jordan already? He is our God at the brink of the Jordan and He will be our God in the Jordan. He will be the same God on the other side of the Jordan. It takes personal faith in God for Him to part the waters of your Jordan. It takes but a step of believing faith. You can cross your Jordan.

Do not be like the rich young ruler who, when he found what was required, lost his desire. The question, then, to all who have come to a Jordan in your life, "Have you lost your desire since you found out what it requires?"

Chapter 9

Preparing to Confront the "Ites"
on the Road to Canaan

"But thus shall ye deal with them; ye shall destroy their altars, and break down their images, and cut down their groves, and burn their graven images with fire."
Deuternomy 7:5

Preparing to Confront the Ites on the Road to Canaan

Chapter IX

The word of the Lord is clear. He speaks in a voice that is unmistakable. It resonates divine certainty and sureness. It came at a time when ancient Israel, for thirty-eight years after they had refused to enter Canaan, remained in the wilderness of Paran and at Kadesh-Barnea, until the old generation died off. They then resumed their journey by a long detour around Edom. Finally they were encamped in Moab, awaiting final instructions to go over and possess the land God had promised to their fathers. It was a most exciting and momentous occasion.

This memorable farewell sermon by Moses to the ancient people of God reverberates down through the corridors of time. No people of God in any age could read these eternal words and not be motivated to press ever onward and ever upward toward the land that lies beyond the Jordan. Jehovah sets certain rules, which, if followed, will safely guide His people into the Promised Land. To the serious traveler in this old unfriendly world, these words leap, as it were, off the pages and into our collective consciousness. In Deuteronomy 7:1–5, we read:

> *¹When the LORD thy God shall bring thee into the land whither thou goest to possess it, and hath cast out many nations before thee, the Hittites, and the Girgashites, and the Amorites, and the Canaanites, and the Perizzites, and the Hivites, and the Jebusites, seven nations greater and mightier than thou; ²And when the LORD thy God shall deliver them before thee; thou shalt smite them, and utterly destroy them; thou shalt make no covenant with them, nor shew mercy unto them: ³Neither shalt thou make marriages with them; thy daughter thou shalt not*

> *give unto his son, nor his daughter shalt thou take unto thy son. ⁴For they will turn away thy son from following me, that they may serve other gods: so will the anger of the LORD be kindled against you, and destroy thee suddenly. ⁵But thus shall ye deal with them; ye shall destroy their altars, and break down their images, and cut down their groves, and burn their graven images with fire."*

Jehovah laid out the task facing ancient Israel after they had successfully navigated the Jordan River. It is insensitive on our part to assume that such a journey throughout the land of Canaan would be easy, even though Jehovah is leading. It would be inhuman if we assume the heart did not, now and then, give way. Hence we have the cheering voice of the great lawgiver grandly uttering, in his one hundred and twentieth year, words to empower the heart. He was showing Israel, in the name of the Lord of hosts, how much more there is to animate them than there can possibly be to discourage and depress them.

He reminds them of His sovereignty when he: (i) bids them look back to past miracles and wonders and to see in them pledges of future help; (ii) shows them how the providential action of God, which was for them, would be against the enemy; (iii) assured them that He would be among them as an ever-present helper and friend; and (iv) points out, though the process of driving out the Ites might be slow, that if it were done more rapidly, it would be attended with great peril from others and unexpected quarters. Now surely we must not pass over a passage like this, which is so full of interest and instruction for our every day life, while presenting to us as it does two distinct lines of thought.

The seven nations of Ites that Joshua and the children of Israel faced after crossing Jordan on their march into rest, the Promised Land, are the same type of enemies that Christians will face today. Certain spiritual power points are apparent in the text. Jehovah guaranteed the passage. Israel was charged with the possession of the land. On the other side of Jordan, the Ites were greater and mightier than they.

The text demonstrates the attitude that the people of God must manifest when these Ites are encountered. And lastly, Jehovah established for them a holy identity, which made them a relevant people, based in their religiosity. It was Israel's religiosity that Jehovah was determined to safeguard. He knew that the virile monotheistic faith of His people would continually be in peril of contamination from the lewd nature worship with immoral gods, prostitutes, goddesses, serpent, cultic doves, and bulls. The Canaanite cults were utterly immoral, decadent, and corrupt, dangerously contaminating and thoroughly justifying the divine command to destroy their devotees (Deut. 20:17).

Later, I will show that the whole Canaan odyssey of ancient Israel is a microcosm of the Christian's journey today. I will postulate that this journey of God's ancient people acts as a very strict caution against all friendship and fellowship with idols, idolaters, false prophets, and all those who would dare array themselves against the plain teaching of God's everlasting word. Further, I will show that those who are taken into communion with God must have no communication with the unfruitful work of darkness.

Israel's Post-Jordan Assignment

The task for all of us who would dare to navigate the Canaan road is clear. Here is the assignment from Jehovah Himself in reference to the post-Jordan enemies of righteousness, the Ites:

1. *Show them no mercy* (vv. 1 and 2)–Bloody work is here appointed, yet it is God's work and, in time and place, needful, acceptable, and honorable.

2. *Jehovah engages to do His part*–It is spoken of as a thing taken for granted that God would bring them into the Land of Promise, that He would cast out the nations before them. No room was left to doubt that resolve. His power is irresistible. His promise is inviolable, and therefore, without question, He will do it.

3. *The enemies of God's people are depicted as being greater and mightier*–They had been long-rooted in this land, to which Israel became strangers. They were more numerous, had men much more accustomed to war. But all of this would not prevent their being cast out before Israel. The strength of the enemies of God's sovereign people magnifies the power of Israel's God.

4. *Jehovah engages them to do their part*–"Thou shalt smite them and utterly destroy them" (v 2). If God cast them out, Israel must not take them in. They must not be taken in as tenants, not as tributaries nor servants. The enemy, the seed of the people of abomination must not be mingled with the holy seed, lest they corrupt them. Better that all these lives should be lost from the earth than the religion and the true worship of God should be lost in Israel.

5. *They must make no marriage with these Ites*–The end result of a matrimonial pact with the enemy, according to Jehovah, would be "they will turn away thy son from following me." Salomon paid dearly for his folly in these matters. In Ezra 9, 10 and Nehemiah 13, we find a national repentance for their sin of marrying strange wives and care was taken to reform. When we look to the New Testament, we find a clear caution not to be unequally yoked with unbelievers (II Cor. 6:14). Among the reasons given for this New Testament prohibition, one stands out to the author: the old

Hebrew adage, "For he that marries with idolaters does in effect marry with their idols."

6. *They must destroy all the relics of their idolatry* (v 5)–Their altars and pillars, grave and graven images, all must be destroyed, both in a holy indignation against idolatry and to prevent infection. One could, without wresting the scriptures, compare this kill-and-destroy concept with the burning of the conjuring books (Acts 19:19).

A Rhema Word Extrapolation

The author takes liberty here to do an extrapolation from the text. The extrapolation represents a theological movement from the logos word to the rhema word. The significance of rhema (as distinct from logos) is exemplified in the instruction and imagery Paul uses when he talks about the sword of the spirit, which is the word of God (Eph. 6:17). The reference here is not to the whole Bible as such, but to the individual scriptures which the spirit brings to our remembrance for use in time of need. A prerequisite for a rhema word is the regular storing of the logos word (Col. 3:16). In a word, the rhema word is the expression of the logos thought.

The post-Jordan cheering words from Jehovah to ancient Israel on their Canaan odyssey, vouchsafes the extrapolation of our modern Canaan odyssey. In the previous section where Jehovah's task was laid out, we are afforded a rhema word. Emerging from this logos thought are the following postulates:

The difficulties of life as anxiously dreaded by us: There will be times on this journey that the Ites will become such a formidable foe that their tenacity will raise questions of anxiousness in our minds. Going in, we are made aware that they will be mightier than we. Such knowledge will and can be detrimental to the Christian who is not serious. It can cause the Christian to fortify himself or it can cause him to shrink back and give up. To cast glances ahead and foresee the danger and difficulties in the distance can be discombobulating.

Our circumstances, with God's assurance notwithstanding, can cause us to cry out, "How shall we get through them?" We do not refer nor infer from the above statement to those who shrink back as having no living faith in God, and who are perpetually giving way to dark and sinful unbelief.

Commensurately, nor do we have in mind or in view those who have not yet been led out of the "house of bondage." But because contextual continuity is crucial in exegeting the rhema word, we refer to those who, through mercy, know what a great deliverance has been wrought for us in Christ Jesus; for those whom that redemption has become a living power through the energy of the Holy Spirit. Yet notwithstanding, we all have our moments of dependency, when by ocular energy we survey the distance, and in our minds eye, see innumerable obstacles confronting us and ask, "How shall we get through them?" The author suggests that, going in, we do not have any idea on how we are going to fare. We do not know the challenge of the process, but if you go through it, by making it with God's help, when you come out on the other side, you will qualify as a tour guide!

These mental propensities of normal human doubt will raise questions and they can take several forms. Here are a few for your consideration:
- How can I know that the ends and aims of my life are achievable?
- How do I overcome the weight and sin that hinders my

ministry to Christ?
- How do I deal with the crooks and bends in my Christian walk with the Lord?
- How do I overcome the personal idiosyncrasies that have hindered my relationship with others?
- How may I vanquish all the foes within and without that threaten the possession of Canaan?

There is not one serious soul on the road to the Canaan of rest who has not, at one time or the other, felt one or more of these inquiries in his spirit and soul, with shivers from the cold of a doubting forecast not withstanding.

The difficulties of life graciously anticipated and provided by God: This power point is a rhema word found implicitly in the words: the Lord thy God. That's the staple statement that ensures and guarantees all that is needed to deal with Ites on the road. In this statement, the Lord thy God guarantees the Canaan traveler that "greater is he that is in you than all they which can be against you." Simply put, it says, "If God be for you who can be against you?" As Jehovah laid out the task before His people, He also assured them:

1. He will go before us to clear the way (7:20). All nature waits on Him: fire, thunder, hail, lightning, flies, worms, locusts, hornets; all must give obeisance to Him. Even the satanic host from hell and the angelic host of heaven must do His share of work when He calls.

2. He will be with the Canaan traveler, to empower him in the way (7:21). If God is on our side, there is power, whatever the seeming weakness. If God is not on our side, there is but weakness, whatever the seeming power.

3. He will choose His own best methods of helping us in the way (7:22). He knows the best method, therefore His sovereignty must be recognized. He knows at what rate we should travel. Once He chooses the rate of our travel, a more or less rapid rate would bring disaster to the traveler. God will gently clear our way.

4. It is God's choice and His secret that causes us to meet and grapple with things and beings mightier than we are. The divine intent is to ensure that we cease to rely on ourselves and come boldly to Him for strength. The human tendency toward self-trust and self-laudation is one of our strongest flesh propensities. This is what we alluded to earlier, and called it the process. It is through the process of our Canaan odyssey and the difficulties in life that molds and makes us.

The way in which we meet these difficulties and how we respond to God's way of dealing with us while confronted with them, exist so we are educated for eternity. If on this journey all were smooth, if we had no complications to meet, no trials to bear, we will become woefully unprepared for the constant attack from the Ites on the road.

It is by these lulls, breaks in our peace, and kinks in our armor, that we are drawn closer to our God. They teach us to want Him, and show us how incomplete we are without Him. The fact of the matter is, we have entered and started out on this journey, and the supreme question that demands recognition is not "Will it be smooth or rough?" but "How will it end?"

Clearly, the rhema word assures us, we have a very special honor conferred on us. We are chosen unto holiness, chosen to be ministers of God's righteousness. On this Canaan journey, our

God condescended to enter closer alliance with us, designed to be called our God and take our interests into His care. As long as we keep His commandments, He will keep His covenant.

The seven nations of Ites were greater and mightier than Israel, yet they will fall before the holy people of God. Clearly this ancient story was written for our learning. It says to us, if we would persevere, with God's help, purity shall eventually disperse power. Right is genuine might. Holiness has, by divine appointment, an everlasting tenure. So the call is rise up and fight! Fight the Ites!

We must not rest until we are sure that every "Ite" is defeated, and there remains no place for them to rest their feet. If we can only realize that God is on our side, we shall be confident of victory. His omnipotence is never exhausted. It is impossible for God to be inconsistent with Himself. The key is to be absolutely sure of the promises of God. It will then be in that assurance that we persevere forward and ever onward, setting at defiance every fear and, without fear or favor, calmly face every foe. We can fight and defeat the Ites on the road to Canaan. We have but only to rub the drowsiness from our eyes of unbelief that we might see the token of God's presence on every side.

Those of us on the Canaan road must travel with a particular mindset. If yours is a secular Canaan or a spiritual Canaan, the mindset is the same. Nothing or no one must be allowed to hamper, hinder, or handicap your travel. The demand is to develop a tough mind while maintaining a tender heart. We must develop tunnel vision, and anything or anyone not going our way, or who will not enhance our ability to continue our forward progress, must be rejected. The will must be developed that permits us to say "no" and feel no pain. Whatever or whoever it is that will deter, delay, or disengage us from the vision must be exterminated. This goes to the question of the state of our mind. We have a commission to allow nothing to prevent us from possessing our Canaan.

When the Israelites were preparing to cross over into Canaan, they were directed to exterminate the seven nations of Ites they would find there. That was their commission. The possession of the land of Canaan was to be conducted upon that principle. From this principle we get the following rhema word.

Nations, like individuals, may become incorrigible: There can be no doubt that sin tends to find and become an incorrigible condition if the divine mercy is not accepted and allowed to exercise its undermining power. The nations of Ites that Israel was to face were manifestly in a hopeless, hapless, and utterly ruined state of being. God regarded them as beyond redemption, and their continuance would only prove pestilential. The purpose of this book is to alert the travelers of the Canaan road to realize this sad possibility.

The Israelites were sent into Canaan to establish the true worship of God: They were not to be ashamed of their religion, but to establish it, and to allow nothing to interfere with it. As Abraham had entered Canaan centuries before as the promulgator of a new religion, so his descendants were to enter into the Promised Land with the view of establishing the religion of Abraham in spite of all possible opposition. As they were to go into the land of Canaan, so are we.

There must not be any thought of sharing with the modern day Ites of Canaan. Such thoughts will only endanger our religious faith. Many of our young have thought that they could associate with irreligious non-Christians, and even marry them, in the hope of bringing them to a better way of thinking.

History records that such hope and entanglements are generally disappointing. The apostle Paul admonishes us, clearly, that such ventures are to be rejected (II Cor. 7:14). To not reject secularism, modernism, and denominational entanglements would be tantamount to allowing the pestilence to propagate itself. Israel's commission was clear: *"Exterminate these incorrigible Ites, or by their seductions they will lead you to your destruction at the hands of a just God"* (v. 4).

On our journey today we are similarly and aptly warned. In Col. 2:8, we read:

> *"Beware lest any man spoil you through philosophy and vain deceit, after the tradition of men, after the rudiments of the world, and not after Christ."*

In Paul's letter to the young man Timothy, in I Tim. 6:12, we read:

> *"Fight the good fight of faith, lay hold on eternal life, whereunto thou art also called…"*

In our next chapter, we will meet face-to-face these enemies. The process of possessing the possession will begin. Going in, Israel knew that she was going to have to fight. How she came out was determined by how well she had internalized the "Rules of the Road."

Chapter 10

Confronting the "Ites" on the Road to Canaan

"And be not CONFORMED to this world, but be ye TRANSFORMED by the renewing of your mind."
Rom. 12:2

Chapter X

The seven enemies referred to as Ites in this volume, which Joshua and the children of Israel faced on their journey into Canaan, are the same enemies faced by every child of God today. As shown earlier, God prefaced their journey with the admonition that "they are greater and mightier than thou." Therefore, it is only by God's grace that Israel could defeat them. To do this, two things must be apparent: Israel must have a steadfast mindset and believe God was leading them on every level.

Commensurately, we must fight. We must hoist the sword of the Spirit. We must be strong in the power of His grace. The battle is the Lord's. From the Divine logos, I will extract the rhema word. To do that I will explain the etymological denotations and connotations of the nomenclature of the seven Ites. As you probably know, Bible names reflect character: Abram—exalted father; Peter—a stone; Barnabas—son of consolation; Jacob—deceiver, supplanter; and so on. Conversely, some of the meanings of the names of these seven spirits can be inferred by a description of their nature. I will show that the connotation of Israel's enemies is the same as our enemies. For example, in a word the Hittites were Israel's enemy, but fear, dread and terror, the connotation of the Hittites derivative, are our enemies!

Hittites: "Fear, Anxiety, Worry"

This designation connotes the spirit of "fear, dread, and terror." This fear was caused by the fierceness of the Hittites. Fear is a spirit that has dogged the Christian continuously. There are 365 commands in the scriptures to fear not, be not afraid, fret not thyself, and be careful for nothing, and so on. Is this a significant number? Certainly so! Every day of our lives, we need to be reminded to not fear or worry—have faith! In Hebrews 11:6, we read:

> *"But without faith it is impossible to please him: for he that cometh to God must believe that he is, and that he is a rewarder of them that diligently seek him."*
> (Emphasis mine)

One of the most common problems that keeps Christians from maturing and enjoying the blessings of the Christian life is the matter of fear or worry. Many Christians worry about many things all the time. In fact, it seems that many Christians have forgotten the warning of the Lord to "make no covenant with them." Some Christians are not happy unless they are miserable! It is clear to me that worry is a sin! In Matt. 6:25, we read:

> *"Therefore I say unto you, Take no thought for your life, what ye shall eat, or what ye shall drink; nor yet for your body, what ye shall put on. Is not the life more than meat, and the body than raiment?"* (Emphasis mine)

To worry then, is to break the command of the Lord. This Ite will consume us and immobilize us if we do not attack and defeat it out of our lives. But the familiar quote: "Fear knocked, faith opened the door and there was no one there," reminds us to continue in the faith and continue to put our trust in God.

What is fear? Fear is a spirit of anxiety caused by a real or imaginary danger. Anxiety is worrying about what might happen. The Hittites sent fear and dread into the hearts of their common enemies. Fear differs from dread.

Fear is a mental reaction to what has the possibility of happening while dread is a mental reaction that immobilizes and paralyzes one in the face of danger. Against this Ite, God assures us that we can overcome this enemy (Ps. 23:14; 27:1, Ecc. 12:13). How do we overcome this enemy? This spirit that paralyzes and immobilizes us from the work of ministry? In Ps. 37:5, we read:

> *"Commit thy way unto the Lord; trust also in him; and HE SHALL BRING IT TO PASS."* (Emphasis mine)

> *"Many are the affliction of the righteous: but the Lord delivereth him OUT OF THEM ALL ({Ps. 34:19).*
> (Emphasis mine)

Winning one's battle against the Hittites does not mean the war is won. Don't quit! There will be many battles; however, the Lord will have the victory. He will deliver you out of them all! If you are sharing space with the Hittites, it is time to attack! Make no further covenant with them. Demand, in the name of Jesus, to be released from the spirit of fear, dread, and terror! Develop this mindset as you read this page; there are four things God cannot do:

1. God cannot fail
2. God cannot lie
3. God cannot die
4. God cannot be pleased without faith

Knowing and believing this, and when you internalize this, resolve to fight! Fight fright! Fight the spirit of the Hittites! (See II Timothy 1:7)

GIRGASHITES: "DWELLERS ON THE SAFE SOIL"

These Ites are satisfied to be "dwellers on the safe soil." These resolve to remain on the other side, at the borders of the mature Christian life, instead of entering the land that flows with milk and honey, a land that is so plentiful that it flows with bounty. They decided to remain on the safe soil. They have considered the cost of crossing over to discipleship and determined that they are not willing to pay the price. They chose rather to walk by sight.

A mountain man was confused when he heard a politician repeatedly mention the "status quo" in his speech. So he turned to his friend and asked, "What does that word stay-tus-kwo mean?" His friend pensively scratched his head and said, "I think stay-tus-kwo means the mess we're in." I could add to that an acrostic of the term "mess" it would bring to mind "misery, evil, side by side!" There are Christians today who have decided to stay in "the mess they are in." It is an "old one more night with the frog's mentality" that was indigenous of Israel in Egypt. How many Christians do you know who having been baptized and saved by the blood of Jesus, but then refuse to move away from the boundary of the former world from which they came?

There are Girgashites spirits in the church whose sole purpose is to keep other Christians from getting involved in ministry. Their sole purpose is to create in the minds and hearts of other unsuspecting Christians a do-nothing attitude toward enlarging the borders of the Kingdom of God. How many times have you seen these Girgashites rise up mightily and show themselves, especially during a building program period? How many times have you seen these Ites rise up to fight against progress and truth of the book gospel preaching? These Girgashites will lay low until the church has a real need or a valid reason to move forward, whereupon they raise their ugly heads and campaign for the status quo. They enumerate how long a certain method, ministry, or model has existed, and how foolhardy it would be to seek change.

We are living in a changing world, a changing culture. We, however, are not a "cultural church," but rather a "church in the culture." The early church, as we see it in the first century, was "counter-cultural." Culture's folkways and mores must not be allowed to become part of the church worship simply because they are cultural traits.

To the Girgashites, tradition is law, and if it's law, it must be tradition. They see any change as mutiny! This is the spirit of the Girgashites. They do not want anything set in that they cannot predict. In their mode of thinking, they would be at their homes on Sunday morning, yet they want to be able to look at their watches and predict exactly what's transpiring at church—the reason being that the church has not changed the order of service in twenty-five years! The Hebrew writer urges us to "keep running, and run to win." Keep "looking" unto Jesus who is "the author and finisher of our faith." To this concept, Jesus spoke clearly. In John 17:14, we read:

> "I have given them thy word; and the world hath hated them, because they ARE NOT OF THE WORLD, even as I am not of the world." (Emphasis mine)

The prolific apostle Paul speaks to this issue, and gives us a rhema word in the process. In Phil. 4:13, we read:

> "Brethren, I count not myself to have apprehended but ONE THING! Forgetting those things which are behind and reaching forth unto those things which are before." (Emphasis mine; paraphrased)

Again the prolific Paul gives a backhand lick to the modern Girgashites. In Rom. 12:2, we read:

> "And be not CONFORMED to this world, but be ye TRANSFORMED by the renewing of your mind."
> (Emphasis mine)

The key word in the text is "transformed." This term, transformed, is a translation of the Greek term "metamorphoo." It is from this term that we get our English word metamorphic. The term metamorphic mean to change in appearance, character, condition, and/or function. The rhema word would be "you cannot stay the same!"

Robert Kennedy in Indianapolis, Indiana, on the night of Martin L. King, Jr.'s assassination, said regarding Dr. King: "Some people see things as they are, and ask why; others see things as they never were, and ask why not." This is an apt description of Dr. King, the apostle of social change, in my opinion.

The spirit of the Girgashites must be destroyed. We cannot convenant with them. We must destroy their altar places, because they are antagonistic to God's will and God's way for our lives on the Canaan road. It is the spirit of the Girgashites that will have you believe, "what will be, will be, so there is no need to pursue Canaan." The Girgashites will seek to get you to believe that, because nothing good has ever happened to you, therefore nothing good will ever happen to you. Once you accept this mindset, you are then suspicious of anything good ever being good.

This attitude leads to a vigorous defense of the status quo. Canaan becomes a mirage, a fantasy, a figment of an imagination gone wild, and not to be believed. That being so, Canaan road travelers must fight. Fight the spirit of the Girgashites! Again, we defer to Paul. Paul was a Canaan road traveler. When we observe Paul from the Damascus road to the Roman road, we see a life of struggle, but not giving an inch to the Girgashites' spirit on his Canaan odyssey. In II Cor. 11:23–28, we read:

> "²³...in prisons more frequent, in deaths oft. ²⁴Of the Jews five times received I forty stripes save one. ²⁵Thrice was I beaten with rods, once was I stoned, thrice I suffered shipwreck, a night and a day I have been in the deep; ²⁶In journeyings often, in perils of waters, in perils of robbers, in perils by mine own countrymen, in perils by the heathen, in perils in the city, in perils in the wilderness, in perils in the sea, in perils among false brethren; ²⁷In weariness and painfulness, in watchings often, in hunger and thirst, in fastings often, in cold and nakedness. ²⁸Beside those things that are without, that which cometh upon me daily, the care of all the churches."

What a résumé! The more you love the Lord, and the more the Lord favors you, the greater the suffering experienced from within and without. The Ites on Paul's Christian odyssey seem to have represented a concerted effort of Satan and all his hellish imps to prevent him from reaching his Canaan. Regardless of these attempts, Paul reached his Christian odyssey! He reached it because "he believed God." In II Tim. 4:6–8, we read:

> "⁶For I am now ready to be offered, and the time of my departure is at hand. ⁷I have fought a good fight, I have finished my course, I have kept the faith: ⁸Henceforth there is laid up for me a crown of righteousness, which the Lord, the righteous judge, shall give me at that day: and not to me only, but unto all them also that love his appearing. (Emphasis mine)

The Journey to Canaan

This Pauline soliloquy, notwithstanding his struggles, should energize all of us on the Canaan road. For it says to us, if we are diligent and dutiful, the God who cannot fail or lie will bequeath to us our rightful inheritance. With this mindset, we set out to fight. We fight stagnation, procrastination, inertia, and status quoism and "look unto Jesus who is the author and finisher of our faith." The hymnologists Natalie Merchant and Karen Peris were correct when they wrote:

> There's a land beyond the river
> That they call the sweet forever
> And we only reach that shore by faith's decree
> One by one we'll gain the portals
> There to dwell with the immortals
> When they ring the golden bells for you and me
>
> Don't you hear the bells now ringing
> Don't you hear the angels singing
> 'Tis the glory hallelujah Jubilee
> In that far off sweet forever,
> Just beyond the shining river
> When they ring the golden bells for you and me
>
> We shall know no sin or sorrow
> In that heaven of tomorrow
> When our hearts shall sail beyond the silvery sea
> We shall only know the blessing
> Of our Father's sweet caressing
> When they ring the golden bells for you and me
>
> Don't you hear the bells now ringing
> Don't you hear the angels singing
> 'Tis the glory hallelujah Jubilee
> In that far off sweet forever
> Just beyond the shining river
> When they ring the golden bells for you and me

> When our days shall know their number
> When in death we sweetly slumber
> When the King commands the spirit to be free
> Nevermore with anguish laden
> We shall reach that lovely Eden
> When they ring the golden bells for you and me
> When they ring the golden bells for you and me

Fight! Fight the spirit of the Girgashites! (I Tim. 6:12)

Amorites: "Mouthy, Talkers"

Another of the Ites that ancient Israel had to face was the Amorites. The connotation of this name means "a sayer, a talker." James, the half-brother of our Lord, said that the Christian who could control his or her tongue or speech was "perfect" (meaning fully developed, mature). There are at least two things that must be understood about the sins of speech. Speech has two aspects that we need to consider: talk is cheap, and talk is costly!

1. Talk is cheap!

Some Christians are only talk. They have a ten million-dollar testimony but back it up with a ten-cent life. In Matt. 15:8–9, we read:

> "⁸This people draweth nigh unto me with their mouth, and honoureth me with their lips; but their heart is far from me. ⁹But in vain they do worship me, teaching for doctrines the commandments of men."

On the road to Canaan, a cardinal rule of the road is that one's life and lips should agree. When it does not, we call that person a hypocrite. Too many in our fellowship fit this paradigm.

They talk the talk but they do not walk the walk. If I were to ask the reader to make a sin list cataloging all the sins identified in the New Testament, you probably would be surprised—surprised that the majority of the sins would be speech sins (i.e., lying, boasting, blasphemy, bearing false witness, gossiping, and so on). Perhaps that is why James says, *"And the tongue is a fire, a world of iniquity…it defileth the whole body, and setteth on fire the course of nature; and it is set on fire of hell."* (James 3:6)

2. Talk is costly!

Think of all the harm that has been done by words. You, the reader, can remember the times you have been hurt, embarrassed, or angered by someone's unkind and un-Christian remarks. Many are the scriptures in the canon that speak to the danger of a loose tongue:

Ps. 5:9	*"they flatter with their tongue"*
Ps. 34:13	*"keep thy tongue from evil"*
Ps. 57:4	*"their tongue, a sharp sword"*
Prov. 6:17	*"A proud look, a lying tongue"*
Jer. 9:8	*"their tongue is as an arrow"*
James 3:5	*"tongue is a little member"*
I Pet. 3:10	*"refrain tongue from evil"*

On the Canaan road, we must be careful not to get hung by the tongue. The Amorites were masters of the science of the tongue. They were not as concerned about doing as they were about saying! The beloved John, writing in the Johanine literature of the scriptures, addressed this malady. In I John, we read:

1:6	*"If we SAY that we have fellowship with him, and walk in darkness, we lie…"*
1:8	*"If we SAY that we have no sin, we deceive ourselves, and the truth is not in us."*

1:10	*"If we SAY that we have not sinned, we make him a liar, and his word is not in us."*
2:6	*"He that SAITH he abideth in him ought himself also so to walk, even as he walked."*
2:9	*"He that SAITH he is in the light, and hateth his brother, is in darkness even until now."*
4:20	*"If a man SAY, I love God, and hateth his brother…"*

James, the half brother of the Lord, continued to address the spirit of the Amorites. In James 3:2, we read:

"For in many things we offend all. If any man offend not in word, the same is a perfect man, and able also to bridle the whole body."

How do we fight these Amorites? We fight them by being able to "show and tell" of Christ's love to a lost and dying world. How do we fight the spirit of these Amorites? Defer to Paul's message in Col. 4:6:

"Let your speech be alway with grace, seasoned with salt, that ye may know how ye ought to answer every man."

Fight! Fight the Amorites! Show and tell! Not just tell!

CANAANITES: "DWELLERS IN THE PLAINS, LOWLANDERS"

One of the more interesting Ites we will meet in our efforts to possess our Canaan is the Canaanites. Connotatively, Canaanites were lowlanders, which denotes a geographical location because they lived in the plains or valleys. But this designation was much more than a geographical location, it is an apt description of their character. These Ites of the lowlands had low morals. They were a wicked and carnally minded people making them undoubtedly and naturally a mortal enemy of the ancient people of God.

These Canaanites dwelt in the plains of Nod. Nod, which was built by Cain, was the very first city in the scriptures. It became the home of murderers, rebels, and wicked sinners. Paul, thousands of years later, seemed to have had no problem in using metaphoric nomenclature in describing the character of certain of these Jews. In Titus 1:12, we read:

> *"One of themselves, even a prophet of their own, said, The Cretians are alway liars, evil beasts, SLOW BEL-LIES."* (Emphasis mine)

When we look at our cities in America today, not much has changed. Most big cities are in the lowlands. It can aptly be described as "lowland," and its citizens and residents are fast becoming known as lowlanders. In contrast, Christians are described as mountaineers who, in turn, look askance at lowlanders.

From His experiences, we learn that Jesus was a mountain man. Remember when He called His disciples on a mount and preached one of His greatest sermons—the Sermon on the Mount. He was also transfigured on a mount. He prophesized the future on a mount. He was crucified on a mount. He was buried in, and arose from, a garden tomb on a mount. We also serve a God who is a God of the hills and valleys. This makes Christians mountain people or people of the high road. We walk the high road, for that's the road that Jesus walked. The psalmist, David, knew of mountain experiences. He said, "I will lift up my eyes unto the hills from whence cometh my help. My help cometh from the Lord, which made (the) heaven and earth."

The Canaanites were in the land, the Promised Land, yet they did not live like citizens of that land. Just as there were Canaanites in the Promised Land, so too are they in the church today. No self-aware Christian today should be diluted into believing that all that our members of the kingdom are worshipping Christians. Jesus clearly made this distinction in the parable of the "ten virgins." In Matt. 25:1–12, we read in verses one and two:

> *"¹Then shall the kingdom of heaven be likened unto ten virgins, which took their lamps, and went forth to meet the bridegroom. ²And five of them were wise, and five were foolish."*

Much could be said about these early representatives of the kingdom. In keeping with the theme of this volume, the five wise and five foolish virgins arrest our attention. Clearly, Jesus is saying there is an equal amount of Ites and Christians in the kingdom. No one who has received deliverance in Christ should be overly concerned when they meet Canaanites in the church (land). Persons should not leave the church because of Ites!

We are clearly warned of their presence. In I Cor. 5:1, we read:

> *"It is reported commonly that there is fornication among you, and such fornication as is not so much as named among the Gentiles, that one should have his father's wife."*

Lowlanders! The morals of this church had sunk to its lowest ebb. The church was in full knowledge of this case but did nothing about it. The Ites had taken the ascendancy in this local congregation. Rather than fight the Ites, the members at Corinth were fellowshipping the Ites!

Many are the times new converts get overtaken by the spirit of the Canaanites in a local congregation, and consequently never realize the riches of the grace of God. They never reach the heights of their high and holy calling. They never experience a mountaintop encounter with God. They never learn to pray and fellowship with the Lord. They unknowingly array themselves against God by enlisting in the armies of the Canaanites!

Let's examine who is considered to be a Canaanite. They are those that rob unsuspecting Christians of the spirit-filled life. It is their sworn duty to see to it that all with whom they come into contact live beneath their privilege! They lead our children to the graveyard of life—into the "far country" of secularism and materialism. They lead them to the "hog pens" of life and look with glee as they are reduced to degeneracy as they eat the slop of degradation when all hope is gone. These Canaanites reside are in our land! They are in the church and we commune and worship with them. Don't be bamboozled and bedazzled by their rhetoric. The lesson here is: don't be a carnal Canaanite—be a spiritual saint. Fight the Ites! Fight the Canaanites!

Perizzites: "Squatters, Belonging to a Village"

The Perizzites were known as "squatters, belonging to a village." By definition, a squatter is one who claims rights to what another owns by taking possession of their property. These Perizzites live off others. Their modus operandi is to do nothing, but take credit for everything!

In today's church vernacular, they would be referred to as pew-taters and church bums. They are in church every Sunday, but church is not in them. They do not join themselves to any ministry or committee. They do not give their time, talents, or money to enlarge the borders of the Kingdom of God. This non-Christian behavior results from their determination to not make a commitment or share the burden and responsibility of a ministry. Their goal is to share in the blessing and benefits of the church, but to contribute nothing.

These are the Perizzites who want their name on the church roll, but want to be a delegate, hopping from church to church and visiting a different church every Sunday. Their pet refrain is, "What's wrong with visiting my brother and sisters at other congregations?" That is an excuse to not be under the oversight of a local leadership of elders. They do not leave their lay-by at their local church, nor give in the collection at the church visited.

What these Ites really want is personal city-, country-, and statewide recognition. They want to be a star and, while they may become one, they most certainly will not be the kind of star of whom God approves. In Jude Chapter One, Jude talks about those who:

> "¹⁰...*speak evil of those things which they know not....* ¹¹*Woe unto them! for they have gone in the way of Cain,* ¹²*clouds they are without water, carried about of winds; trees whose fruit withereth, without fruit, twice dead, plucked up by the roots;* ¹³*Raging waves of the sea, foaming out their own shame; WANDERING STARS, to whom is reserved the blackness of darkness for ever.*"
>
> (Emphasis mine)

These Perizzites are also depicted as wanderers, wandering through this Christian journey and living off others. They greedily take credit for work and labors they had absolutely nothing to do with. These wandering stars need to be arrested!

Everyone must make this journey for himself. We must stand in the judgment to give account of the deeds done in "our bodies." We cannot enter into the land of promise riding on someone else's ticket! Squatters and parasites in the kingdom must be rejected, reproved, and rebuked, not joined! Fight! Fight the Perizzites! Don't be a Perizzites' parasite—be a paraclete (a holy spirit)!

Hivites: "Wicked, Guileful, or Hypocritical"

The Hivites were very interesting enemies of ancient Israel. Their name connotes "wicked, guileful, or hypocritical." The following scripture can best illustrate the etiology (cause) and effect of hypocrisy. In Joshua 9:3–20, we read:

> "³And when the inhabitants of Gibeon heard what Joshua had done unto Jericho and to Ai, ⁴They did work wilily, and went and MADE AS IF they had been ambassadors, and took old sacks upon their asses, and wine bottles, old, and rent, and bound up; ⁵And old shoes and clouted upon their feet, and old garments upon them; and all the bread of their provision was dry and mouldy. ⁶And they went to Joshua unto the camp at Gilgal, and said unto him, and to the men of Israel, We be come from a far country: now therefore make ye a league with us. ⁷And the men of Israel said unto the Hivites, Peradventure ye dwell among us; and how shall we make a league with you? ⁸And they said unto Joshua, We are thy servants. And Joshua said unto them, Who are ye? and from whence come ye? ⁹And they said unto him, From a very far country thy servants are

come because of the name of the LORD thy God: for we have heard the fame of him, and all that he did in Egypt, ¹⁰And all that he did to the two kings of the Amorites, that were beyond Jordan, to Sihon king of Heshbon, and to Og king of Bashan, which was at Ashtaroth. ¹⁴And the men took of their victuals, and asked not counsel at the mouth of the LORD. ¹⁵And Joshua made peace with them, and made a league with them, to let them live: and the princes of the congregation sware unto them. ¹⁶And it came to pass at the end of three days after they had made a league with them, that they heard that they were their neighbours, and that they dwelt among them."

(Emphasis mine)

The Gibeonites/Hivites were hypocrites! How many times have you heard or been told, "I'd go to church if it were not for all the hypocrites." The statement is true. We stipulated as much in the section on the Canaanites. One of the problems people poses for themselves—those that make such statements—is their position of inconsistency. There are a number of hypocrites in restaurants, but that does not keep them from going there to eat. Hypocrites are in hospitals, doctor's offices, grocery stores, where they are employed, yet they frequent these places without objections.

As noted in the section on the Canaanites, it is crucial to understand that because people in the church do not live right, that does not adversely effect the efficaciousness of the church. The validity of the one true church is not affected by who may become a member of it. Understand further, people are not perfect, but the one true church is a perfect institution! Lastly, the church is not a museum for saints; it is a hospital for suffering sin-sick souls. People in the one true church are people suffering from soul-sickness-sin!

Let us who love the Lord and have set out on this road to Canaan rid the lost and unsuspecting Christian of his excuse for going to hell. Don't be a Hivite. Practice what you preach. Live what you believe. Fight! Fight the Hivites! Let us open our eyes to awareness of these Hivites, whose sole purpose is to misdirect our focus and cause us to maunder. They seek to get you from looking up to Jesus who is our perfect example and down to people who are woefully imperfect!

Jebusites: "A Threshing Place"

The connotation of this name indicates a "threshing place." A definition of a threshing place is in order. By definition, a threshing place is a trodden-down place because of the specific activities there. After the wheat was harvested it was taken to a threshing place—usually a flat place on a hilltop.

The wheat, stalks and all, would be spread on the ground and then trampled or trodden under foot. This process separated the wheat kernels from the stalks and the chaff. When the harvesters were convinced that the wheat was separated, they manually removed the stalks. They then took a sifting tool, which looked like a large pitchfork, and separated the wheat and chaff by casting the mixture into the air. The chaff, which was lighter than the wheat, was blown away by the wind. The heavier wheat kernels fell directly back to the ground.

When that process was done, the kernels were gathered into baskets to be taken to the market or to the homes. The sifting process was rather strenuous and difficult, but there was no other way for the ancient farmer to easily separate the bad (the chaff) from the good (the wheat).

On the road to Canaan, the Jebusites will take you to the threshing place! The idea is to ascertain if the Canaan traveler has the wherewithal necessary to occupy and possess the Promised Land. They present to the traveler "the process" of the Canaan odyssey. They look for weakness by creating situations and scenarios designed in intent and purpose to cause the child of God to quit the journey. They turn up the heat by asking questions like, "How much can you stand without fighting back?" Every Christian, at one time or another, goes through the threshing floor process, which is a sifting process wherein the chaff is released in his or her life.

Many, on the road to Canaan, have given in to the pressures, trials, and tribulations of the Jebusites' process! Satan is the mind behind the Jebusites; he is the leader of the pack. It is he who desires to have us. He brings us to processes that put our Christianity to the ultimate test.

There are three categories of sifters in the Christian life: (i) persons, (ii) providence, and (iii) possessions. These three are dealt with in the Philippians letter as the three great robbers of joy. We know we will be sifted, but the question is not will we be sifted, but when. Jesus gave Simon Peter good advice during Peter's sifting time. In Luke 22:31–32, we read:

> *"³¹And the Lord said, Simon, Simon, behold, Satan hath desired to have you, that he may SIFT you as wheat: ³²But I have prayed for thee, that thy faith fail not: and when thou art converted, strengthen thy brethren."*
> (Emphasis mine)

With reference to the first sifter, persons: Persons become the "who" in our lives that are difficult to get over in the process to which the Jebusites bring us. In the Roman letter, Chapter 8, Paul asked several questions: *"Who,"* he asks, *"shall separate us from the love of God?"* Notice he did not say "what"! It is not the what(s) of our lives that create real problems for us; it is the "whos," the persons!

Paul also said, "In all these things (meaning the whats) we are more than conquerors." He indicates that we can deal with the whats. Our time of trial comes when there is a who involved. To further clarify this point, consider the verb "lying." Lying, in and of itself, does not necessarily give us a real problem. But being lied to is something we have come to accept in many instances. So it is not that we have been lied to that upsets us, it's who lied to us that upset us!

Many people have left the church, not because of sin, but because of who it was that sinned. Can we get over the whos in our lives? We will be confronted on the road to Canaan by significant whos, ready and willing to deceive us. Can we go on despite the shortcomings of others?

With regards to the second sifter, providence: The term providence, by definition, means under one's control or that which is controlled by one. So when the term providence of God is used, often the user is referring to that which is out of his or her control and under the control of a higher power or deity. Things happen to us as Christians over which we have absolutely no control. How we respond and react to these things can be sifting.

Job was subjected to physical and mental deprivations over which he had absolutely no control. But he was determined to go through the process believing that God was in control. In

Chapter I, we discussed the idea of situations. I sincerely believe that God allows situations in the lives of His people to accomplish His purpose. I further believe that through divine providence we are spared to do the continuing work of God. As Job accepted the providence of God over which he had no control, we must do the same.

With regards to the third sifter, possessions or things: Wealth and possessions are one of the devil's strongest sifters. Paul said concerning things (possessions): "But what THINGS were gain to me, those I counted loss for Christ" (Philippians 3:7). Jesus tells us that the way to have the things we need and to have them be a blessing to us is to "Seek ye first the kingdom of God, and His righteousness; and all these THINGS shall be added unto you" (Matt. 6:33). If Christians would put the Lord first, everything else will fall in place.

Jesus spoke to this same issue. In Luke 12:15, we read:

"And he said unto them, Take heed, and beware of covetousness: for a man's life consisteth not in the abundance of the THINGS which he possesseth."
(Emphasis mine)

How easy it is for today's Christians to get carried away with what the Jebusites bring to the table. We like or appreciate things. We all do, but we all need to be clear as to the direction from which things come. First, things are like prayer. Just as prayer changes people, so too people change things. Some say prayer changes things, but I beg to differ. People must change things. Conversely, we must rid ourselves of the misnomer that things change people. Things are amoral; they do not change people.

Secondly, God does not send physical things to the modern Christian anyway. God sends blessings (James 1:17), and all the blessings He sends are spiritual (Eph. 1:3). When God finds a man or woman He can work through, this is the one person to whom He sends the blessings!

Finally, the Devil is not in the spiritual blessings business. He is in the physical blessings business. He will give you things and delude you into believing that they came from God. This is his methodology. In Matt. 4:1–9, we read:

> "⁸*Again, the devil taketh him up into an exceeding high mountain, and sheweth him all the kingdoms of the WORLD, and the glory of them; ⁹And saith unto him, ALL THESE THINGS will I give thee, if thou wilt fall down and WORSHIP ME.*" (Emphasis mine)

The Devil pays off in worldly things; god pays off (blesses) in spiritual things (blessings). Christians who miss this lesson of the direction from which blessings come will be woefully misled. It is clear that God hears only the prayers of His faithful people. Commensurately, He blesses only those who scripturally worship Him. In James 1:25, we read:

> "*But whoso looketh into the perfect law of liberty, and CONTINUETH therein, he being not a FORGETFUL hearer, but a DOER of the WORK, THIS MAN SHALL BE BLESSED IN HIS DEEDS.*" (Emphasis mine)

There you have it! God blesses the man and the deeds of the man that hears and does His will. So before we get excited about the things that the Jebusites bring to us, tempting us, know that they can clearly be a bribe or reward from the Devil himself.

Do not get caught up in things (possessions). The Messianic Master addressed this question. In Matt. 16:26, we read:

> *"For what is a man profited, if he shall gain the whole world, and lose his own soul? or what shall a man give in exchange for his soul?"*

The Jebusites will bring you to the threshing floor to be tested, tried, and sifted. But we can persevere if we fight! Fight the Jebusites! They can bring us to it, but rest assured God can bring us through it!

Chapter 11

Possessing Canaan's Possessions

"Hear O Israel: thou art to pass over Jordan this day, to go in and possess nations greater and mightier than thyself, cities great and fenced up to heaven."
Deuteronomy 9:1

Chapter XI

One of the greatest tragedies of our religiosity is our not having learned how to possess our possession. Many saints of God have died spiritual paupers when they could have enjoyed the abundant life and died spiritual billionaires. God wants all those who love and obey Him to possess what He has clearly provided for us to possess. When one becomes a Christian, one becomes an heir of all the things of God. In Romans Chapter 8 and verse 17, we read:

> *"And if children, then heirs; heirs of God, and joint-heirs with Christ...."*
>
> *God said to Israel, "I will bring you into the land whither thou goeth..." (Deut. 7:1).*

I call upon every Christian to pay close attention to the "I wills" of the Lord.

The "I Wills" of Christ

Down through the arcade of man's civilization, words have been his cardinal and principal means of communication. Words are rapids of ideas constituting a vehicle conveying thoughts. All that man has ever said to man has been said in words! A man's word is his bond. It is an absolute truism; a man must keep his word. No man living or dead has kept his word as surely as the Messianic Master. When the Master speaks, it shall come to pass! As fellow Canaan travelers, we should not ever have any doubt in our minds about the certainty of the words of the Master. The

The Journey to Canaan

Canaan traveler must be about the business of possessing the "I will" promises of the Master. Without any doubts, there is divinity in His every word. He spoke to this in John 6:63:

> "It is the spirit that quickeneth; the flesh profiteth nothing: the words that I speak unto you, they are spirit, and they are life."

In the latter part of John 6, the text suggests that some of His disciples were having some problems with the tenor and tone of His words. The Master did not change His words. He spoke to those in His inner circle. We note that the Master did not directly concern Himself with those who "went back, and walked no more with Him." He turns to His inner circle and posed a question with finality in it and asks, "Will ye also go away?" The statement is pregnant with what He did not say!

The statement suggested that the Master was not going to change His word. Not even for those in the inner circle was He going to water down His word to get their loyalty. The master was speaking the words of His father. It was His father that gave Him the words of what He should say. The tone of His words, it seems, suggested that determination to Peter. It was Peter who responded:

> "Then Simon Peter answered him, Lord, TO WHO SHALL WE GO? Thou has the WORDS of eternal life."
> (Emphasis mine)

We are sure that the Master had no intent, then or now, to change His word to fit the desire of the masses. In John 12:48, we read:

> *"He that rejecteth me, and receiveth not my words, hath one that judgeth him: the word that I have spoken, the same shall judge him in the last day."*

The words of the Messianic Master will stand throughout all ages to come. The venerable apostle Paul addressed this question in Col. 3:17:

> *"And whatsoever ye do in word or deed, do all in the name of the Lord Jesus, giving thanks to God and the Father by him."*

There should not be any hesitancy on the part of any Canaan traveler to possess our possessions in Christ Jesus. Let me suggest to you, the reader, a few things that we should possess based on the "I will" words of Christ:

1. *"...I will in no wise cast [them] out."* Jno. 6:37
2. *"...I will build my church..."* Matt. 16:18
3. *"...I will send...the Spirit of truth."* Jno. 15:26
4. *"...I will...receive you..."* Jno. 14:3
5. *"...I...will draw all men unto me."* Jno. 12:32
6. *"...I will be with you always."* Matt. 28:29-20
7. *"...I will come again."* Jno. 14:2
8. *"...I will confess you before my Father."* Matt. 10:32
9. *"...I will have mercy."* Matt. 12:7
10. *"...I will give you rest."* Matt. 11:28-29
11. *"...I will never leave you."* Heb. 13:5

Every Canaan traveler can rest assured that we have untold riches of grace that are ours simply by possessing the words of Jesus Christ!

In Chapter I, we showed that Canaan could easily typify any legitimate goal. Canaan is a place, a destination—a place worth striving for. To the evangelist, Canaan is the church, the body of Christ, which the un-churched, the unsaved must reach in order to enjoy the spiritual blessings of the Messiah. Canaan well might represent heaven's many mansions, the final resting place of the soul (presently under construction for all those who love and have obeyed the Lord). Canaan might well be an academic degree, a nursing degree or medical degree, or a degree in jurisprudence.

In the legitimate pursuit of our Canaan one must be forever cognizant of enemies along the road. This cognizance demands a modus operandi to deal with the enemies. We identified in this volume those enemies in Chapter X, and in Chapter I we were given the rules of the road. If such rules are obeyed, total victory will be achieved and our Canaan will be assured.

First and foremost, as explained in an earlier chapter, is the knowledge that God is leading. Chapter III of this volume elaborated on that concept by showing that God, in His second movement in this journey, makes His people a promise. In Chapter II, we saw His presence. He now says, "I will bring you into the land to possess it." God is a God of covenants. He makes a promise and He keeps it, for He cannot lie. In faith and through faith, we must believe the promises of God. There must never be any doubt or fear that what God says will come to pass. Many are the saints of God who live a miserable existence because they fail to possess what is clearly guaranteed by the Holy Spirit. In II Cor. 1:22, we read:

> "Who hath also sealed us, and given the EARNEST [guarantee] of the Spirit in our hearts."
> (Emphasis mine)

He has equipped us with the wherewithal to cross our Jordans and defeat the enemies as we go in to possess our Canaan. We must internalize God's promises through faith, believe them and act on them through faith in His word. In St. John 6:63, we read:

> *"It is the spirit that quickeneth; the flesh profiteth nothing: the words that I speak unto you, they are spirit, and they are life."*

This is how we live the abundant life. The abundant life is lived through the knowledge of the words of the Messianic Master. Internalizing these words and acting on them strengthens us and relieves us of stress, which causes distress. The saint who has possessed his or her spiritual possession is living the abundant life and Canaan is assured.

A Self Concept Mainspring of our Christian Possession

There is a cornucopia of blessings that every saint should internalize at conversion. A knowledge of what we have in Christ goes to the question of a strong Christian concept of self-identification. In the apostle Paul's admonition to the church at Ephesus, he points out the Christian's possession in Christ. In Ephesians 1:3ff, the saints of God are given a list of blessed possessions that are available only at conversion. These must be possessed. At conversion, we have been:

- Chosen (Gk. "eklego")—picked out, selected
- Predestined (Gk. "Proorizo")—predetermined beforehand
- Adopted ("Huiothesia")—a son, a placing, a condition given to one to whom it does not naturally belong

- Accepted (Gk. "Charitoo")—a ready reception of what is offered
- Redeemed (Gk. "Exagorazo")—denotes to buy out, to buy back, bought
- Forgiven ("Aphiemi")—past sins blotted out, omitted
- Made holy (Gk. "Hagios")—separated from sin, consecrated to God, sacred, sanctified.

This is who we are in Christ Jesus. These blessings are not reserved for a certain group, they are available to every soul who, by faith, accepts and obeys the gospel of Christ. God said to Israel, "I will bring you into the land, but you must possess… the land." I have heard saints praying for peace. But peace is not a virtue that God sends down from heaven each time we need it. In St. John 14:27:

> "Peace I leave with you, my peace I give unto you: not as the world giveth, give I unto you…."

Blessed peace is a possession that is maintained and internalized by the saint on a daily basis through faith in His Word. The aim of this volume is to show that to the degree that we possess these possessions, it is to that degree that we will reach our Canaan. God said, "I will bring you." We must not only hear those words, they must be believed, internalized and acted upon.

Life's Storms Versus Our Christian Possessions

An example of hearing but not internalizing (i.e., not possessing the words of the Master), is seen clearly in the episode of the calming of the storm by the Master in a boat on the Galilean sea. In Luke Chapter 8 and Verse 22, we read:

Possessing Canaan's Possessions

> *"Now it came to pass on a certain day, that he went into a ship with his disciples: and he said unto them, Let us go over unto the other side of the lake. And they launched forth."*

The text under consideration clearly indicates and demonstrates that Jesus told the disciples, "Let us go over to the other side." It is clear, also, that the disciples did not internalize the words of the Master even though they heard His words. The power point in the text is "Let us go over to the other side."

NINE THINGS YOU SHOUD KNOW ABOUT STORMS

On their way to the distant shore, a storm arose. This episode indicates that believers can be actively involved in the Master's work, and duly following divine instructions, and all hell will still break out! A believer does not have to be in rebellion or disobedience of the Master for storms to occur in his or her life. Storms will come! They will come in our lives and rob us of our possessions we have in Christ, so we need to know some things about storms. Storms come into our lives because of three reasons (Acts 27:9–25):

1. Because of wrong advice of experts (v 11)
2. Because of wrong advice of the majority (v 12)
3. Because of wrong reading of the circumstances (v 13)

When storms come into our lives they cause us to make at least three mistakes. The three mistakes we make when storms occur are:

1. We drift (v 15)
2. We discard (v 18)
3. We despair (v 20)

The Journey to Canaan

This ancient story is pregnant with storm information. In addition to teaching us why storms come and the mistakes we make when they come, we are wisely afforded the rules that should be followed when storms do come into our lives.

Lastly, we see demonstrated in the text the rules for handling our storms and the wherewithal we have in order to handle them. Three facts we have in the storm are:

1. God's Presence (v 23)
2. God's Purpose (v 24)
3. God's Promise (v 25)

There is a story that provides us a rhema word about storms and our attitude toward them.

An ocean liner was caught in a terrible storm. It seemed that at any moment the sea-worthy vessel would capsize. As one of the passengers sought safety, he saw a small child sitting in the middle of the ship's dining room, playing with a toy. The child seemed oblivious to the chaos and confusion around him. Frantically, the passenger ran up to him and screamed, "You better put on your life vest and find your parents; we're in the middle of a terrible storm!"

The little boy looked up at the stranger and calmly replied, "Thank you, mister, but I am not worried. My daddy is the captain of the ship."

There are people who question how you can keep on believing when everything is turning against you. There may be some who wonder how you can hold your head high when your world is crashing all around you. Yet others may wonder how you can keep smiling when you are going through the toughest storms in your life. What the non-Christians do not know or realize is that Christians have a sixth sense. This sixth sense is called faith. From this internalized faith—which is one of the Christian's possessions—we go to our God in prayer.

What the Christians cannot handle in our physical environment, we turn over to God in prayer. He is the captain of our salvation. Prayer enables. It enables us to believe the unbelievable and achieve the impossible. Prayer has transformed sighs into songs, gloom into glory, burdens into blessings, sadness into gladness, and tragedy into triumph. The old adage is true: When you don't know what to do, pray. Prayer before and during a storm is one of the greatest resources the Christians have. In fact, our deeds will be in direct proportion to the intensity and persistence of our discipline to prayer. Prayer is not something we do for the Creator, necessarily, but for ourselves. It is not a position, but a disposition; it is not all an asking, but a knowing. While we can leave the place of prayer, we do not leave His presence.

In this divine anatomy of our personal storms, we are provided spiritual guidelines for handling our midnights and our personal storms, and possessing our possessions. It is clear that the disciples did not internalize or activate the rules for handling their negative circumstances. They did not internalize the words of the Master. They heard the words but they did not "possess" the words. The words from the Master were:"Let us go over to the other side." Because they had the words, they should have known that no earthly or natural phenomenon could override or cancel the words of the master. If Jesus said, "We are going to the other side," do the math! They would get to the other side!

Saints of God all across our brotherhood and nation are victimized by their circumstances because they fail to internalize the words of the Master by faith in His words. The provisions and possessions received at our conversion must be spiritually possessed. If the saints of God would possess and internalize the blessings that ensue, to every person that would dare to obey God, "self-esteem" would result.

Psychological minutia, psychological literature, or psychobabble need not be consulted to arrive at a state of self-esteem and personal identification. The plain and simple teaching of the holy writ tells us how to think. If saints of God would apply the standard set down by the Holy Spirit for abundant living, we would then be mentally aggressive in carrying out the mandate of the great commission. To the degree that ancient Israel was able to internalize and possess the presence, purpose, and promises of God, it was (as we have seen) to that degree that they would be able to reach and claim Canaan, the land that flows with milk and honey.

Concurrently and commensurately, saints today must learn how to possess their possession, the absence of which will cause spiritual apathy and niggardliness in our support and spread of the glorious gospel of Jesus Christ. From this divine proposition and postulate, there can be no successful rebuttal.

Relevancy and Identity—A Christian Crisis

When saints of God fully possess the possessions that are ours, it renders moot the crisis of relevance and identity that plagues the modern Christian. The modern Christian who has not internalized and activated by faith what is received at conversion fights against that which makes him relevant as a child of God.

Jesus understood His "relevance" as a priority; therefore, His identity did not impede His dedication to His purpose. As a matter of fact, Jesus said, "I came not to call the righteous, but sinner to repentance." To the degree that He did this, it was to that degree that He was relevant. He was brutalized and hung on a tree. The people said, "If thou be the son of God come down from the cross and we will believe you." But relevance to Jesus was staying on the cross, for it was "for this purpose," he said, "came I into the world."

Not knowing how to handle relevance and personal identity causes us to waver and stagger at the promises and purpose of our God. Jesus loved sinners and God loved sinners. God loved sinners so well that He gave to them His only begotten son. Jesus loved sinners so well that he died for their sins and gave them the church. How dearly and intensively do we love sinners? Do we go where the sinners are to teach them about the love of Jesus? Do we turn up our noses at sinners? Are we uncomfortable in the presence of sinners? Not because we fear for our lives, but because we do not want other saints to misidentify us.

Which is more important: our relevancy, made so by our divine message, or what others may think of us if we carry that message into certain quarters? Do we talk to a prostitute or a known drug dealer on the streets of our city, or do we pass them by for fear of misidentification? We can only break through these crises when we fully internalize who we are and what we are spiritually created to be. It is only when we fully internalize by faith that we are chosen, accepted, adopted, forgiven, redeemed, made holy and without blame before Him in love, that personal identify become irrelevant and our witnessing to the un-churched becomes that which makes us relevant.

I challenge you to do a study of "what we have in Christ" using Ephesians 1:3–7 as the text. What will emerge, if you are serious, is a fundamental treatise for Christian self-esteem. It is possible for the modern-day Christian to read the riches of grace and come away unchanged and feeling irrelevant or vice versa.

The story of "the good samaritan" is a case in point. It shows us how this man possessed a sense of altruism, an altruism that said, "What is important is not what will happen to me if I help this man but, if I don't help him, what will happen to him." He was not only possessed with a sense of altruism, but his was even a dangerous altruism—dangerous, because he could have been misidentified as one of the robbers. It is therefore crucial and fundamentally important that the modern day Christian learn from the Deuteronomic story of the ancient people of God on the ancient page the absolute necessity of possessing our possession in the claiming of our Canaan.

There will be times in our struggle to possess our Canaan that we will feel alone. Aloneness is a malady that can be both frustrating and depressing. If you are experiencing any of these feelings, be encouraged; there is a provision. It is what I call hitch-hiking or "thumbing." In the next chapter, this necessary Canaan road method of travel is explained.

CHAPTER 12

Hitchhiking

on the Road to Cannan

"And the things thou has heard of me among many witnesses, the same commit thou to faithful men, who shall be able to teach others also."

Chapter XII

As you have seen, the journey into Canaan is a struggle, a warfare, long and tiring. We now see clearly that Canaan is a process. The final goal through it all is possessing it as your Promised Land. What could be more exciting?

Along the road to Canaan where we engage the enemies, fight indefatigably and laboriously, we are afforded some milestones—milestones that are drenched with the blood, sweat, and tears of the greats that have gone on before, and are now in the grandstand of eternity. From that vantage point they cheer us, reminding us we, too, can make it.

Yet at times, this grand old road to Canaan seems endless and at other times pointless. Yes, there will be moments when we will sit down by its side in abject dejection. It will be in those moments that we will wonder why we ever bothered setting out in the first place. Yes, it is a long and lonely road. At times there will be no one on it to which we can go for comfort and advice. We will find, at times, that there will be no one on this road that will take the time to listen to our sorrows, let alone comfort us in them. Most of us are guilty of thinking thoughts like that at one time or another.

Even though the realities of the Canaan road are inevitable, there is another dimension we have not addressed. At the very beginning of this section, I mentioned the greats that have gone on before us. Though gone, there is much to be said by their legacy. They have experienced the lows and highs of the Canaan road. They developed ways of coping with tiredness, cynicism, jealousies, and downright waywardness they encountered on their Canaan journey. Their markers and milestones are stained with their blood, sweat, and tears. Many of them did, however, manage to pass on their experiences and insights to those who followed.

Most of my contemporaries in the gospel are grateful for those great soldiers who graciously passed the baton to us. They not only passed the baton, they passed information to us. They were generous in passing to us biblical arguments that have stood the test of time in the forensic arena. Therefore we do not feel alone; we are surrounded by a great cloud of witnesses (Heb. 12:1–2) who are shouting their encouragement and advice to us as we fight the good fight!

We see these great warriors of days gone by as purveyors of wisdom. We must make the best use of this wisdom—wisdom that has been quarried from the living stone of past lives of faith and tested on their journey to Canaan. While I cannot speak for others, I can speak authoritatively about myself. I am convinced that, in addition to the Rules of the Road, to succeed in any endeavors one may choose, certain lessons must be learned. One lesson for sure is learning how to hitchhike or thumb.

Thumbing a Ride

As I write this section, my spirit is transposed to the land of my nativity. In Valdosta, Georgia, in the early years, we called it "thumbing." Thumbing to us meant getting a ride with someone else who is going your way. We believed that thumbing was an acceptable means of transportation, especially when the culture accepted it and allowed it.

During the decades of the sixties and seventies, thumbing was part and parcel of the patois of our culture. The hitchhiker was usually a solitary soul without a mobile means, who stood on the side of the road seeking a pick-up from some friendly driver. Usually truck drivers were favorably disposed in picking up the hitchhiker.

In a later personal biographical sketch I will enlarge this concept. In the sketch, I will show in minute details how I successfully hitchhiked my way into a successful Christian ministry. Hitchhiking is a biblical concept (II Tim. 2:1–2). I have been blessed beyond measure in my Christian walk with the Lord mainly because I was able to hitchhike with others who were blessed to have hitchhiked with others before me.

My ministerial heritage is, in my opinion, unique and different, and represents a strong biblical bloodline. My ministerial roots reach all the way back to Marshall Keeble. It was Marshall Keeble who taught and baptized Luke Miller. Luke Miller taught and baptized John H. Clay. John H. Clay taught and baptized me! I was doubly blessed in that I was able to personally travel with and meet each of these great soldiers of the Canaan road. But by no means were these the only giants of the faith who allowed me to hitchhike and impacted my life and ministry. I had the unique privilege to meet, travel with and live with men like James L. Cothern, Ulysses Shields, William Whitaker, and V.E. Williamson. In my autobiography, I will list others like S.T.W. Gibbs, Jr., who taught me much more than even he himself knows.

Hitchhiking is an apt paradigm of Christian spirituality, for it is a tacit yet strong reminder that we do not have to be alone on this Canaan road. It reminds us further that we do not have to rely solely on our own personal wherewithal, but we can successfully hitchhike with others who have been this way before. We can hitch a ride with someone else!

Hitchhiking or "thumbing" offers yet another dimension. It allows us to not only get a free ride, but it affords us company along the way. It allows us to share with those who are going the same way we are going. Secondly, we find ourselves at the end of the ride closer to our destination than when we started. To thumb a ride is to learn more about people and life, as well as moving along the Canaan road to our Promised Land.

To hitchhike is to learn from others. As you ride with them, soak up those things that made them successful. Pay attention to their story of history. Relish in their handling of situations. Be attentive until they drop you off. Having been dropped off, you can then begin to use the acquired knowledge to forge ahead on the Canaan road. While a previous ride may have been most helpful, you must not be totally oblivious to hitching another ride with someone else.

God in His grace allows and provides others able to help and sustain us on the Canaan road. Even if not in person, we can still ride with the greats of yesteryear. We can ride with them through reading, reflecting on their writings; we can ride alongside them. In the process of the ride we can absorb their wisdom, taking great comfort from the fact that they chose to undertake the same walk of faith as ourselves.

Their arguments, dissertations, means of coping, and theses were developed over a lifetime of wrestling with the rich resources of the Christian faith and the realities of the spiritual life. Their efforts are to our benefit. We can absorb the wisdom of a lifetime as we ride and walk along with them. When the baton is passed to our generation, we will find that their fight is still our fight and their dreams are our dreams.

The image of the hitchhiker is on point. It assures us we are not alone on this journey to Canaan. Blessed are those of us who have lived to touch the legends of yesteryear. To have been able to sit at their feet, learning from their ideas and examples, encouraged and affirmed by their presence, is more than enough! The time is now to hitch a ride with someone who has wrestled with the issues of being sojourners in the world and exiles from our homeland. One day the evils will be over, ended, and we who have walked in victory and righteousness will be home at last!

Anselm of Canterbury (c. 1033–1109) interprets a longing for God in exile in three different, yet clearly related ways:

1. Our present situation is that of being orphaned or being in exile—that is, separated and cut off from a full knowledge of God. We sense the pain of separation.

2. The realization that we are in exile helps us to appreciate that we are in the world but not of the world. The world is not our homeland; it is our place of exile and we must look beyond it, while nevertheless appreciating whatever beauty it may possess and attempting to make it a better place. We are sojourners in this land, not permanent residents.

3. This realization encourages looking forward with eager anticipation to finally being in the radiant and glorious presence of God and beholding His face.

Anselm helps us to understand our situation of being hitchhikers, orphans, and exiles on the Canaan road. We will not be able to find the ultimate joy and satisfaction that we seek on the Canaan road. So we welcome the anticipation of the rides we may secure with others along the road. Yet we are assured of what awaits us at journey's end and are encouraged to long for this even more.

THE HITCHHIKER AND KOINONIA

Life on the road to Canaan can be difficult, frustratingly hard and disconcerting. But because we can hitchhike, we know we do not have to travel by ourselves. Part of God's provision for us is that to provide fellow travelers and companions along the road, the intent of which is to motivate, encourage, and build us up in the most holy faith. Fellowship, the Christian Koinonia, is not an afterthought, neither is it a luxury we can take or leave. It is an absolutely necessary spiritual condition that is fundamentally important to our travels on the Canaan road. Fellowship is foundational to our Christian growth. We are biologically and spiritually constituted by God so that companionship is vital to our physical, mental, and spiritual growth.

The denotation of the term fellowship indicates the act of mutual sharing. Fellowship is a two-sided coin or a dual-level experience: on level one, we have fellowship with the Divine; on level two, we have fellowship with each other. In the Epistle of I John 1:3, 7, we read:

> "³That which we have seen and heard declare we unto you, that ye also may have FELLOWSHIP with US: and truly OUR FELLOWSHIP is with the FATHER, and with HIS SON Jesus Christ. ⁷But if we walk in the light, as he is in the light, we have FELLOWSHIP one WITH ANOTHER, and the blood of Jesus Christ his Son cleanseth US from all sin." (Emphasis mine)

The fundamental and foundational idea in the Christian Koinonia is that the saints of God on the Canaan road enjoy a dual experience. We receive spiritual energy from Christ on the one hand and with other believers on the other. The latter is a means of deepening the former. The question as to why may arise. Why is Christian association so important on the road to Canaan? Is there any room for solitude at all? Actually, if I am not careful here, I may give the impression that solitude is antagonistic to Christian fellowship. That, of course, is not my intent. I am fully cognizant that being alone allows us to pray and reflect. How many times during the ministry of the Messianic Master did He withdraw to a solitary place to pray? Solitude on the journey permits us to claim space to reflect and meditate.

There is a decisive difference between our time of fellowship and short periods of meditative reflections. Extended periods of solitude can adversely affect our times of fellowship with others of like faith. Too much time to oneself on the Canaan road can lead directly to depression, discouragement, and introversion. We must see ourselves as a community on the march. At times we will stop to rest, pray, and reflect.

The nation of Israel—the motif for the Canaan odyssey—is seen as the community of God forging its way toward Canaan. Sometimes its movement is slow and sometimes painful. At one interval its forward travel was delayed forty years. Their dream was deferred forty years. Yet when the order was given to "Head 'em up, move 'em out," they obeyed!

Hitchhiking is therefore allowed. Hitchhiking allows us to have fellowship with other traveling companions on the Canaan road. Hitchhiking with men and women of like faith can deepen our faith. It can serve us as a network of support. God allows great men and women of God to come our way. We must not be hesitant or intimidated to thumb a ride. Many have allowed jealousy, envy, and strife to keep them from thumbing a ride with those who have come through and over many toils and snares. Oh, the lessons we miss and the experiences we lose because of the green eyes of jealousy, envy, and strife!

The Veracity of Thumbing

There is truth, accuracy, and precision in the process of thumbing and hitchhiking. The church, the redeemed community of God is pictured as a "body" in scripture (I Cor. 12:12–31). In Romans 12:4, we read:

> *"For as we have many members in one body, and all members have not the same office."* (Emphasis mine)

It is clear that all members in the body of Christ do not have the same office, but all have an office. We all have and play different roles. A careful reading of the context suggests that we may not all be an ear or an eye—but someone in the body is! The blessing of this text demonstrates to us that the forward movement of the church on the Canaan road is corporate. It is corporate and diversified in gifts, and its abilities enable us. This truth causes each traveler to recognize his or her weakness without guilt. Where I might be weak, another might be strong. In this case hitchhiking and theological thumbing is allowed.

On this journey, we can benefit from the gifts and talents of others. The strength and courage of others can cover our shortcomings and weaknesses. Those who come in contact with travelers who are weary and thumbing along the Canaan road must be willing to pick up those travelers and allow them to ride as far as you can take them. Fellowship is not merely about giving, it is about receiving as well. In Paul's dissertation to the church at Corinth, in his first letter, he reminds them of this fact. He tells them that spiritual gifts are given for the "edification" or the "building up" of the church in the most holy faith.

This is a salient point, which I will explore in another volume. For the purpose of this discussion, I will say this: our gifts, whatever they may be, are not given for entertainment—to make us some kind of secular provocateur—to elicit some kind of spiritual thrill. Our gifts in our service to God have a deadly serious function. They are to be used to elevate and motivate people to see Jesus and not us! They are to be used to bring the hearts of the people into direct confrontation with Christ. Our gifts should be used as if Christ was using them Himself. If what we do in our service and worship to God only bring attention to ourselves, it is a misuse of a God-given gift! Whatever we do, if it is not to uplift Jesus, it is a personal performance and not worship!

Those who are new to the Canaan odyssey should know that there are those on this road who have been through what they are going through. When you have the opportunity, hitchhike! Thumb! They may be the ones who just might be able to make sense of what you are going through. There is no person on the Canaan road that has not, at one time or the other, hitchhiked. There must be a certain pathos that identifies us as travelers. Every traveler should be willing to share a ride with whoever seeks a lift on this journey.

All of us who have traversed this road for some time have experiences to share. Some are good and some bad, relatively speaking. Those who are the pioneers on this road must be willing to tell others who thumbed or hitchhiked a ride with them what the Lord has done and is doing in their lives. The reasons we need to share with others are varied. Many become tired and weary as they travel and desperately need support. Each traveler must realize that those who are strong today may be weak tomorrow.

On the Canaan road, we are linked together by a common goal and a common destiny. We also have a common enemy seeking to keep us from crossing our Jordans and possessing the land of promise. Let us not be hesitant to hitchhike on our road to Canaan. Where the opportunity presents itself, to thumb or hitchhike, do it! It may be with a close friend in Christ, a family member, or your local minister. Do not be afraid to lean on their shoulders when there is a bona fide need.

Horatius Bonar, in his discussion of suffering said, "Suffering is inevitable in this 'vale of tears.'" He said, "It is an immense consolation to know that others have known it before us, and felt its pain."

"The path of sorrow is no unfrequented way. All the saints have trodden it. We can trace their footprints there. It is comforting, nay; it is cheering to keep this in mind. Were we cast-fettered into some low dungeon, would it not be consolation to know that many a martyr had been there before us; would it not be cheering to read their names written with their own hands all around the ancient walls? Such is the solace that we may extract from all suffering, for the furnace into which we are cast has been consecrated by many a saints already."

The image offered by Bonar is important. The footprints of the saints are imprinted on the road of faith ahead of us. In journeying, we are following behind them, sharing their experiences and sorrows, just as we shall finally share their joy at entering through the gates of the Promised Land.

Epilogue

"We need to believe and embrace as a certainty that our Promised Land—our new Jerusalem—lies beyond the borders of our earthly lives, and live out that life in the sure and certain knowledge that our Promised Land lies before us—awaiting our entrance.
—**Alister McGarth**

Epilogue

In our day, there are many misunderstandings surrounding the Christian life. We are living in an age when even gospel preachers are caught up in a theological frenzy to make the Christian life easier and more acceptable to the world.

While this book primarily deals with biblical coping that is experienced on the road to Canaan, its meaning is clear. The Christian life is not an outing or a walk in the park. This journey that we started when we received our deliverance is a never-ending battle! We enlisted in the army of God. We are engaged with a spiritual enemy who is far more powerful than we are (Eph. 6:12). On our own and in our own strength, we are not a match for the old Devil!

The good news, however, is that he is no match for the God we serve. Against God, he is powerless (I John 4:4). Why? Because we serve a living and all-powerful Savior. When the battle rages, we are confident of victory (Rom. 8:31, 37). The fact of the matter is, the word informs us that we are recipients of victory through the Lord Jesus Christ (I Cor. 15:57). There is a mindset that every Christian must have when enlisted in the army of God and our engagement in the battle with evil Ites. Victory is ours and, because victory is ours, we can walk in victory every day on the road to Canaan.

What began at the call of Abraham to leave his place and people and set out for an unknown destiny blossomed into the vocation of Moses. Moses was to lead his enslaved people out of the god-haunted ambience of cyclical Egypt—a construct where everything had to be answered, set in stone like the staring immobile statues of Pharaoh. From these two journeys we have gone from the person (the destiny of Abraham), to the corporate (the destiny of people of Israel). We have gone from a personal god (a household god that one carries along for good luck), to YHWH (the God of gods), whose powers are mightier than even the mightiest power earth can summon. Taken together, these two great escapes give us an entirely new sense of the past and the future—the past as constitutive of the present and the future as truly unknown.

But what of today's present? Is it just a moment, glinting briefly between past and future, hardly worth elaborating? No, it is to be a pulsing, white-hot center of all the subsequent narrative, the unlikely intersection of time and eternity, the moment where God is always to be found.

We have seen the weaknesses and the strengths of the ancient people of God. We have observed the skill and devotion of this people through all their history to revere the past without adoring it. We have observed them before the opaque mystery of the future without offering it the fear that is reserved to God alone. We have seen them at their best and at their worst. From this story of the Canaan odyssey we must conclude that the road to Canaan demands that we must neither stand in the storied past, nor the imagined (or dreaded) future, but firmly in the pregnancy of the present moment!

This is a story of an evolving consciousness, a consciousness that went through stages of development and that, like all living things, sometimes grows slowly and at other times in great spurts. We must, if we believe the Bible to be true, believe that the experience on which this story is based is inspired. I would hope that the case is mutual with the readers of this volume. The evolution of the consciousness of the ancient people of God, taking place as it did over so many centuries, was animated and kept warm by the spirit and breath of God. The story of the road to Canaan is one of a nomadic people over and across the millennia against seemingly impossible odds. It can also be viewed as a unique microcosm of cultural survival. The Canaan story shows us how we too, with an unwavering faith in God, can experience a whole new reality in coping with the stresses of life. If one seriously wishes to observe the finger and hand of God in the human condition, it can most certainly be found here.

One cannot and should not come away from this story and brush aside, as merely human expressions, absence of the supernatural work of God. We must see that in the post-Exodus experiences, the deep meaning of our own individual lives. It is almost impossible to imagine the great liberation movements of modern history without reflecting on the early people of God as recorded in the Hebrew Bible.

One cannot imagine the reality of the abolitionist movement, the civil rights movement, the movement of indigenous and dispossessed peoples, the anti-apartheid movement in South Africa, without some knowledge of the story of the road to Canaan. In all these movements the proponents have used, to some degree, language of the emancipation of the ancient people of God. Readers of this volume must decide if the movement of God in the lives of early Israel speaks to us today. In the book of Hebrews 12:1-2, we read:

> *"¹God, who at sundry times and in divers manners spake in time past unto the fathers by the prophets, ²Hath in these last days spoken unto us by his Son, whom he hath appointed heir of all things, by whom also he made the worlds."*

If the reader is convinced, there will be no question of needing proof, any more than we require proof of anyone we believe in. For in the final analysis, one does not believe that God exists any more than one believes that Timbuktu exists. Our job is to believe in God, as one believes in a friend—or one believes in nothing! That this is the case, I refer you to Hebrews 11:6:

> *"But without faith it is impossible to please him: for he that cometh to God must believe that he is, and that he is a rewarder of them that diligently seek him."*
> (Emphasis mine)

The whole argument comes down to whether one believes in God. God is a faith fact. Everything comes down to faith in Him. Such a faith is fundamentally important to our navigation of the Canaan road.

The intent throughout this volume is to get Canaan travelers to pause and reflect on how the great God of Israel undergirds all our values and that, without Him, all our human efforts are doomed to certain failure. The venerable apostle Paul spoke to this question in Romans 15:4. We read:

> *"For whatsoever things were written aforetime were written for our learning, that we through patience and comfort of the scriptures might have hope."*

We see this concept played out in the vision of Isaiah's vision. He articulates that true faith is no longer confined to one nation, but all nations. All nations, he said, "shall flow into the house of YHWH that He may teach us of His ways." He teaches us in various and sundry ways; sometimes through dead ends, detours, and dry places.

Epilogue

The Canaan road is there. It is there to be traveled. If it could not be mastered, it would not be there! There will be those along the way who will discourage you, ridicule you, and humiliate you, but master it—you must. Edgar A. Guest said in his poem "It Couldn't Be Done":

> Somebody said that it couldn't be done,
> But he with a chuckle replied
> That "maybe it couldn't," but he would be one
> Who wouldn't say so till he'd tried.
> So he buckled right in with the trace of a grin
> On his face. If he worried he hid it.
> He started to sing as he tackled the thing
> That couldn't be done, and he did it.
>
> Somebody scoffed: "Oh, you'll never do that;
> At least no one ever has done it";
> But he took off his coat and he took off his hat,
> And the first thing we knew he'd begun it.
> With a lift of his chin and a bit of a grin,
> Without any doubting or quiddit,
> He started to sing as he tackled the thing
> That couldn't be done, and he did it.
>
> There are thousands to tell you it cannot be done,
> There are thousands to prophesy failure;
> There are thousands to point out to you, one by one,
> The dangers that wait to assail you.
> But just buckle in with a bit of a grin,
> Just take off your coat and go to it;
> Just start to sing as you tackle the thing
> That "cannot be done," and you'll do it.

The Journey to Canaan

Moses did not reach Canaan, but he saw it. He died knowing that God's promise and was there, a true reality. He died knowing that God's promises could be trusted and that others would eventually enter into the promised inheritance of the people of God. He now knew what he had up to now believed; that is, he had placed his trust in God who is trustworthy.

We do, from time to time, want to be sure that the Promised Land is really there. In the New Testament case with Simeon, the older man who, we are told, longed for the "consolation of Israel." When his dim and tired old eyes fastened upon the child Jesus, he knew then that he could die in peace. God's promises had been fulfilled (Lk 2:25–32).

We want our doubts to be vanquished and thrown to one side. Yet we have to learn to live with them without letting them drag us down. Nobody making that long journey from Egypt to Canaan really knew for a certainty that there was, in a real sense, a Promised Land. But they resolved that what they had been promised outweighed all the weariness of the journey there.

We are promised eternal life in the New Jerusalem. We have never seen its gates or walls. We can hardly imagine what it will be like. Yet this New Jerusalem is heeded before us as the Promised Land was to ancient Israel. Our task is to begin to anticipate our joy in entering into it. The intent of this volume was to get the readers to enter into the biblical text and anticipate the experience of entering the New Jerusalem.

One of the most prolific writers of the Middle Ages was Bernard Cluny (c. 1100–c. 1150), who used powerful visual imagery to stimulate reflection on the consummation of the journey. Notice how Bernard draws a parallel between the New Jerusalem and Canaan through imagery. If you are making a long journey to see someone you love, the goal of your journey is going to have a major effect on your behavior. The goal is the motivating force why the journey began in the first place. That goal does not stop you from pulling over to the side of the road if you see someone get hurt. It does not mean that you treat the wonderful people you meet along the way with contempt or pay no attention to the beauty of the country you are driving through. All these things are appreciated, but are seen in their context. Wonderful though they may be, journey's end is even more sublime. Allowing our thoughts to dwell dreamily upon our future hope reaffirms its reality and increases our sense of longing to be there and enter into its fullness.

He states further, "Life on earth can be transformed by the hope of life in the New Jerusalem." Because of what our Canaan portends, our lives and daily living can be transformed by what Canaan can bring—joy and gladness. If today we allow our hearts and minds to dwell on our future destiny, we will then have the necessary and required essentials to achieve the right perspective on where we are and where we are going.

All of us who have embarked on the Canaan road would do well to remember the words of Martin Luther: "Whatever your heart clings to and confides in, that is really your god."

So, is our heart really set on our future glory? Or are we locked into earthly things that prevent us from grasping and claiming as our own the great promise of God to His people? These questions pose a powerful challenge to our way of thinking and the values that implicitly shape our lives.

If we have lost our spiritual vision on this Canaan road, maybe the suggestions presented in this volume on the hitchhiker is appropriate. Maybe we should try "thumbing." Seek out someone on the Canaan road who is going the right way and seek encouragement, solace, advice, and instructions from them.

We can rest assured that Canaan far surpasses the bleakness, darkness, and drabness of this earthly life. It is so much better than what we are experiencing and will transform and transcend anything and everything we currently know. With this faith we gear up for the journey of life. With this thought, we continue on our journey, knowing that its end is not far away. At last we will see the one whom we have longed to meet face-to-face. Perhaps it is too much for our mortal minds to perceive.

About the authoR

Dr. W.F. Washington, Sr. has been the full-time pastor of New Golden Heights Church of Christ for 27 years. During his tenure in the Fort Lauderdale area, he was elected as Great Personality of the South in 1974; selected Minister of the Year by radio station WRBD in 1976 and 1989; founded the Golden Heights Multi-Crisis Center in 1991; founded the Golden Heights Christian Academy in 1992; selected and served on Broward County Economic Council by Commissioner Ilene Liberman in 1992; and was recently selected as Minister of the Year by Delevoe Foundation in 2000.

In 1960, Dr. W.F. Washington served as minister of the Westside Church of Christ in Marshall, Texas; Director of Student Employment, Bishop College, Dallas, TX; and Dean of Men at Bishop College, Dallas, TX. In 1962, he was Dean of Students and Director of all Non-Academic Affairs at Bishop College, Dallas, TX. In 1965, he was Assistant Principal for Administration at Pemberton High School, Marshall, TX. Finally in 1968, he became the full time pastor at Westside Church of Christ, Marshall, TX.

Dr. Washington's published works include: Can You Run With Horses; The Church on a Collision Course; Is God Black; When You Have Lost a Love One; The Christian and Stress; The Christian and Depression and Now That I am a Christian. His unpublished works include his Ph.D. dissertation on the topic: "Do Lower Class Black Commit Suicide More Frequently Than Whites in a Homicidal Mode Due to Cultural Orientation and Role Engulfment"; "Religiousity, the Answer to Juvenile Delinquency"; "How Shall the Young Secure Their Heart"; and "The Key to Growth in the Black Church".

His past honors and commendations include: listed in Who's Who Among Students in American Universities and Colleges in 1960; Youngest Dean of Students in Black Universities and Colleges in 1961; elected President of NAACP and one of the defendants in the NAACP landmark case: "The Marshall Nine" in 1963; elected to serve on the Missionary Board of the Monrovia Foundation, Monrovia, Africa in 1971; and selected to the Board of Trustees of Southwestern Christian College, Terrell, Texas in 1980.

Dr. Washington's educational degrees include a Ph.D. in Behavioral Psychology, an M.S. in Criminal Justice and Contemporary Corrections and a B.S. in History and Western Civilization.